QUICK SUPPERS

Canadian Living's™ best

BY

Elizabeth Baird

AND

The Food Writers of Canadian Living Magazine
and The Canadian Living Test Kitchen

A MADISON PRESS BOOK

PRODUCED FOR

BALLANTINE BOOKS AND CANADIAN LIVING™

Ballantine Books
A Division of
Random House of
Canada Limited
1265 Aerowood Drive
Mississauga, Ontario
Canada
L4W 1B9

Canadian Living
Telemedia
Communications Inc.
25 Sheppard Avenue West
Suite 100
North York, Ontario
Canada
M2N 6S7

Canadian Cataloguing in Publication Data

Quick suppers

(Canadian living's best)
Includes index.
ISBN 0-345-39807-6

1. Suppers.   2. Cookery, Canadian.
I. Title.   II. Series.

TX738.B35 1996   641.5'3   C96-930807-6

™Canadian Living is a trademark owned by
Telemedia Communications Inc. and licensed by The Madison Press Limited.
All trademark rights, registered and unregistered, are reserved worldwide.

EDITORIAL DIRECTOR: Hugh Brewster
SUPERVISING EDITOR: Wanda Nowakowska
PROJECT EDITOR: Beverley Sotolov
EDITORIAL ASSISTANCE: Beverley Renahan
PRODUCTION DIRECTOR: Susan Barrable
PRODUCTION COORDINATOR: Donna Chong
BOOK DESIGN AND LAYOUT: Gordon Sibley Design Inc.
COLOR SEPARATION: Colour Technologies
PRINTING AND BINDING: St. Joseph Printing Limited

CANADIAN LIVING ADVISORY BOARD: Elizabeth Baird, Bonnie Baker Cowan,
Anna Hobbs, Caren King

CANADIAN LIVING'S™ BEST QUICK SUPPERS
was produced by Madison Press Books
which is under the direction of Albert E. Cummings

Madison Press Books
40 Madison Avenue
Toronto, Ontario, Canada
M5R 2S1

Printed in Canada

Contents

Introduction

"Supper's on the table!" There's no other cry that gathers so many people around the table so quickly. And while the invitation hasn't changed in the nineties, the planning and the preparation of this important meal certainly have.

Let's face it, all of us — from working parents to on-the-go school-age children and busy stay-at-home moms — would love to arrive home at the end of the day and find a delicious supper ready and waiting. With *Canadian Living's Best Quick Suppers*, it's not only possible — it's easy and it's fun.

Possible, because almost all the recipes can be made, from start to finish, in under 30 minutes. Easy and fun, because everyone pitches in.

Call this cookbook our culinary survival kit for today's busy households. Every appealing recipe features short ingredient lists and streamlined step-by-step cooking instructions that do away with a sinkful of pots and bowls. We've also included lots of timesaving shortcuts, shopping tips and menu suggestions — plus make-ahead dishes that save on shopping and cooking during the week. And because all our recipes follow *Canada's Guide to Healthy Eating*, you can be sure every one of our quick-to-make main dishes meets your family's important nutritional needs.

Best of all, every recipe in *Canadian Living's Quick Suppers* is so easy to follow — and so in tune with today's tastes — that younger members of the household will want to lend a hand, or tackle a dish on their own. There's no better inspiration for young cooks, and no better satisfaction. After all, isn't that what sharing supper in the nineties is all about?

Welcome to the table. Supper's ready!

Elizabeth Baird

Chicken with Sage, Tomatoes and Lemon (recipe, p. 17)

Chicken — Yes, Please!

Today, chicken is so plentiful and versatile that we can have it any night of the week. Boneless breasts are great pleasers, but thighs have our approval for flavor, cost and speedy preparation. Here are some inspiring chicken dinners — as well as some turkey delectables, in recognition of turkey's growing popularity and year-round availability.

Chicken and Cheese Enchiladas ▶

Corn tortillas have a wonderful earthy taste and are the most authentic way to package an enchilada.

Per serving: about
- 290 calories
- 12 g fat
- good source of calcium
- 23 g protein
- 24 g carbohydrate
- excellent source of iron

1-1/2 cups	cubed cooked chicken	375 mL
4 oz	cream goat cheese (chèvre) or light cream cheese, softened	125 g
Half	sweet red pepper, chopped	Half
4	green onions, sliced	4
1/2 tsp	ground cumin	2 mL
1/4 tsp	each salt and pepper	1 mL
8	corn tortillas	8
1-1/2 cups	mild salsa	375 mL

● In bowl, combine chicken, goat cheese, red pepper, half of the green onions, the cumin, salt and pepper; set aside.

● In steamer or sieve set over boiling water, cover and steam corn tortillas, four at a time, for 3 to 4 minutes or until limp.

● Using tongs, arrange first 4 tortillas in single layer on work surface. Quickly divide 1/2 cup (125 mL) of the salsa among tortillas, spreading to edge. Arrange half of the chicken mixture in line down center of each; roll up. Repeat with remaining tortillas.

● Place enchiladas, with sides touching, in greased 13- x 9-inch (3 L) baking dish; completely cover with remaining salsa. Bake in 400°F (200°C) oven for 15 to 20 minutes or until heated through. Sprinkle with remaining green onions. Makes 4 servings.

TIPS

● Look for corn tortillas next to the larger flour tortillas in the freezer or refrigerator section of your supermarket. If corn tortillas are unavailable, divide the filling among flour tortillas and omit the steaming step.

● The trick with corn tortillas is to make them pliable enough to roll up. Traditionally, they are given a quick dip in hot oil until limp, but steaming works just as well and doesn't add any fat.

Oven-Fried Chicken

Natural bran adds fiber, Parmesan cheese provides taste and bread crumbs make the crispness that coats affordable chicken legs. Pop small baking potatoes and quartered acorn squash into the oven before tackling the chicken.

Per serving: about
- 290 calories
- 23 g protein
- 12 g fat
- 24 g carbohydrate
- good source of calcium
- excellent source of iron

1/4 cup	each dry bread crumbs, natural bran and freshly grated Parmesan cheese	50 mL
1 tsp	dried marjoram	5 mL
1/2 tsp	each salt and pepper	2 mL
1	egg	1
4	chicken legs, skinned	4

● In shallow dish, combine bread crumbs, bran, Parmesan cheese, marjoram, salt and pepper. In separate shallow dish, whisk egg with 1 tbsp (15 mL) water.

● Dip each chicken leg into egg mixture, then into crumb mixture, rolling to coat evenly.

● Place chicken on greased baking sheet; bake in 375°F (190°C) oven for 30 to 35 minutes or until juices run clear when chicken is pierced. Broil for 3 to 5 minutes or until golden brown. Makes 4 servings.

REMOVING SKIN FROM CHICKEN

Removing the skin from chicken legs cuts back on fat and takes just seconds to do yourself. With a sharp knife, nick the skin at the foot of the drumstick; insert the tip of the knife under the skin and slit lengthwise. Using a small piece of paper towel to grip the skin, pull it off and discard.

Cajun Chicken Thighs

A blend of peppery paprika, hot cayenne, dry mustard and thyme lends a Cajun zing to chicken.

Per serving: about
- 200 calories
- 23 g protein
- 7 g fat
- 11 g carbohydrate

1 tsp	dried oregano	5 mL
1 tsp	each paprika and dry mustard	5 mL
1/2 tsp	each pepper and dried thyme	2 mL
1/4 tsp	each salt and cayenne	1 mL
1/4 cup	buttermilk	50 mL
1-1/3 cups	whole wheat or soda crackers	325 mL
8	chicken thighs, skinned	8

● In small bowl, combine oregano, paprika, mustard, pepper, thyme, salt and cayenne. Pour buttermilk into shallow dish.

● In food processor, or in sealed plastic bag and using rolling pin, crush crackers to make fine crumbs. In separate shallow dish, combine crumbs with half of the spice mixture.

● Sprinkle each chicken thigh with remaining spice mixture. Dip into buttermilk, then into crumb mixture, rolling to coat evenly.

● Place chicken on greased baking sheet; bake in 375°F (190°C) oven for 30 to 35 minutes or until juices run clear when chicken is pierced. Makes 4 servings.

TIP: Air-chilled chicken, easy to spot because its dry pale-yellow skin is so unlike the wet white skin of water-chilled chicken, is worth the extra few cents it costs per pound. It cooks up with more flavor and tenderness and shrinks less.

Dijon Herb Chicken Thighs

2 cups	corn cereal flakes	500 mL
1/4 tsp	pepper	1 mL
3 tbsp	light mayonnaise	50 mL
2 tbsp	Dijon mustard	25 mL
1 tbsp	lemon juice	15 mL
1 tsp	each dried thyme, savory, basil and crumbled rosemary	5 mL
8	chicken thighs, skinned	8

● In food processor, or in sealed plastic bag and using rolling pin, crush cereal to make fine crumbs. In shallow dish, combine crumbs with pepper.

● In separate shallow dish, stir together mayonnaise, mustard, lemon juice, thyme, savory, basil and rosemary.

● Dip each chicken thigh into mayonnaise mixture, then into crumb mixture, rolling to coat evenly.

● Place chicken on greased baking sheet; bake in 375°F (190°C) oven for 30 to 35 minutes or until juices run clear when chicken is pierced. Makes 4 servings.

Light mayonnaise mixed with mustard is great for holding the crispy cereal coating on chicken thighs. Keep the rest of the supper simple by serving a plain pasta, such as rotini, with green beans or a carrot-and-cabbage slaw.

Per serving: about
- 225 calories
- 22 g protein
- 8 g fat
- 15 g carbohydrate
- excellent source of iron

Mint Chicken Thighs

1/2 cup	dry bread crumbs	125 mL
1 tsp	dried mint	5 mL
1/4 tsp	each salt and pepper	1 mL
1/3 cup	low-fat plain yogurt	75 mL
1	clove garlic, minced	1
1/2 tsp	grated lemon rind	2 mL
8	chicken thighs, skinned	8

● In shallow dish, combine bread crumbs, mint, salt and pepper. In separate shallow dish, stir together yogurt, garlic and lemon rind.

● Dip each chicken thigh into yogurt mixture, then into crumb mixture, rolling to coat evenly.

● Place chicken on greased baking sheet; bake in 375°F (190°C) oven for 30 to 35 minutes or until juices run clear when chicken is pierced. Broil for 1 to 2 minutes or until golden. Makes 4 servings.

Fresh or dried mint adds wonderful flavor to chicken. This recipe uses dried mint, but if you prefer fresh — and spearmint is the best of the fresh — just triple the amount to 1 tbsp (15 mL) chopped.

Per serving: about
- 195 calories
- 24 g protein
- 5 g fat
- 12 g carbohydrate

ABOUT OUR NUTRIENT ANALYSIS

To meet nutrient needs, a moderately active woman 20 to 50 years old needs about 1,900 calories, 45 g protein, 60 g fat and 250 g carbohydrate daily. Men and teenagers usually need more.

● The analysis was carried out using imperial measures. Calculations were based on the first ingredient listed when there was a choice and did not include any optional ingredients. Nutrient values were rounded to the nearest whole number and calories to the nearest five.

● Calculations of meat and poultry products, including those where fat or skin was not removed before cooking, assumed that only the lean portion was eaten.

● Analysis is provided for calories, grams of protein, fat and carbohydrate and, when applicable, includes good or excellent sources of iron and calcium, and high or very high amounts of dietary fiber.

Portuguese Barbecued Chicken ▲

For the best take-out chicken, find a churascuria — a Portuguese barbecue shop specializing in chicken. This easy homemade version lets you re-create all that amazing, slow-crisping flavor, in your own backyard.

Per serving: about
- 325 calories
- 33 g protein
- 19 g fat
- 3 g carbohydrate

1/3 cup	dry white wine	75 mL
1 tsp	grated lemon rind	5 mL
3 tbsp	lemon juice	50 mL
2 tbsp	tomato paste	25 mL
1 tbsp	olive oil	15 mL
1/2 tsp	paprika	2 mL
1/4 tsp	each salt and hot pepper sauce	1 mL
2	cloves garlic, minced	2
2 lb	chicken pieces	1 kg

● In shallow glass dish, combine wine, lemon rind and juice, tomato paste, oil, paprika, salt, hot pepper sauce and garlic. Add chicken, turning to coat well. Cover and refrigerate for at least 4 hours or for up to 24 hours, turning occasionally.

● Reserving marinade, place chicken, meaty side down, on greased grill over medium heat; close lid and cook for 10 minutes. Turn and cook, brushing with marinade, for 30 to 40 minutes or until juices run clear when chicken is pierced. (Or bake at 375°F/190°C for 30 to 35 minutes, brushing once with remaining marinade.) Makes 4 servings.

TIP: For toting to a cottage or campsite for a potluck barbecue, marinate this Portuguese-style chicken, then stash it, well iced, in a cooler to grill on arrival.

Ginger Chicken

1/4 cup	light soy sauce	50 mL
1/4 cup	dry sherry or apple juice	50 mL
1 tbsp	minced gingerroot	15 mL
1	clove garlic, minced	1
1/4 tsp	each salt and pepper	1 mL
4	chicken legs, skinned	4
1 tbsp	granulated sugar	15 mL
2 tbsp	finely chopped green onion	25 mL

● In shallow glass dish, stir together soy sauce, sherry, ginger, garlic, salt and pepper. Add chicken, turning to coat well. Cover and refrigerate for 12 hours, turning occasionally.

● Strain marinade, discarding ginger and garlic. Place chicken, meaty side down, on greased grill over medium-high heat; close lid and cook, turning often, for 15 minutes.

● Stir sugar into reserved marinade. Brush over chicken; cook, brushing often with marinade, for about 15 minutes or until browned and juices run clear when chicken is pierced. Serve sprinkled with green onion. Makes 4 servings.

*F*resh gingerroot easily lasts for a week or two wrapped in towels, enclosed in plastic and stored in the crisper — so Asian-inspired dishes, such as this grilled chicken, can be as spur of the moment as dishes calling for onion or garlic.

Per serving: about
● 180 calories   ● 27 g protein
● 5 g fat   ● 5 g carbohydrate

TIP: To keep gingerroot fresh and crunchy even longer, peel the root by scraping, as with new potatoes or carrots, and store in a jar filled with sherry. Cut off what you need for a dish and resubmerge the remainder in the sherry. Use the sherry in stir-fries and marinades where a touch of ginger is welcome.

Rosemary Chicken

1 cup	fresh bread crumbs	250 mL
1/4 tsp	each salt and pepper	1 mL
1/3 cup	low-fat plain yogurt	75 mL
1 tsp	crumbled dried rosemary	5 mL
1/2 tsp	grated lemon rind	2 mL
4	boneless skinless chicken breasts	4

● In shallow dish, combine bread crumbs, salt and pepper. In separate shallow dish, stir together yogurt, rosemary and lemon rind.

● Dip each chicken breast into yogurt mixture, then into crumb mixture, turning to coat evenly.

● Place chicken on greased baking sheet; bake in 350°F (180°C) oven for about 20 minutes or until chicken is no longer pink inside. Broil for 2 minutes or until golden brown. Makes 4 servings.

*R*osemary is a blessing to cooks. Pair it with lemon to add incredible savoriness to chicken as well as fish and lamb.

Per serving: about
● 175 calories   ● 29 g protein
● 2 g fat   ● 7 g carbohydrate

TIP: Spiky rosemary needles need to be crumbled finely so they can release their flavor in a short cooking time. When using fresh rosemary, add two to three times as much as the dried variety, depending on your affection for the piney herb.

Ginger Chicken and Green Onion Kabobs ▲

Chinese sauces such as oyster and hoisin are wonderfully convenient for quick marinades. Most grocery stores now sell a selection, and an opened jar can be kept in the refrigerator — ready at a moment's notice to flavor poultry and meat.

Per serving: about
- 160 calories
- 3 g fat
- 27 g protein
- 5 g carbohydrate

9	green onions	9
3 tbsp	oyster sauce	50 mL
2 tsp	minced gingerroot	10 mL
1-1/2 tsp	each vegetable oil and water	7 mL
1 lb	boneless skinless chicken breasts	500 g
1	lemon or lime, cut in wedges	1

● Finely chop white and most of the green part of 3 of the green onions to make about 1/4 cup (50 mL); place in small bowl. Stir in oyster sauce, ginger, oil and water; set aside.

● Cut remaining green onions into 1-inch (2.5 cm) lengths. Cut chicken into 1-inch (2.5 cm) cubes. Alternately thread onions and chicken onto metal skewers. Brush with all of the sauce mixture.

● Place skewers on greased grill over medium-high heat, or under broiler; close lid and cook, turning once, for about 6 minutes or until chicken is golden brown and no longer pink inside. Serve with lemon wedges to squeeze over top. Makes 4 servings.

Sweet and Easy Curried Chicken

2 tbsp	frozen orange juice concentrate, thawed	25 mL
1 tbsp	liquid honey	15 mL
2 tsp	curry powder or paste	10 mL
1/4 tsp	salt	1 mL
4	chicken breasts	4

● In small bowl, whisk together orange juice concentrate, honey, curry powder and salt. Gently lift skin away from chicken, leaving skin attached at bone. Brush all but 1 tbsp (15 mL) orange juice mixture over meat; replace skin over breast.

● Place chicken on foil-lined baking sheet; bake in 375°F (190°C) oven for about 25 minutes or until no longer pink inside. Remove and discard skin.

● Brush chicken with remaining glaze; broil for about 3 minutes or until golden brown and glazed. Makes 4 servings.

You never have to worry about dry chicken breasts again with this recipe from the Test Kitchen. You're guaranteed plenty of taste — and healthful eating, too!

Per serving: about
• 175 calories   • 27 g protein
• 3 g fat   • 8 g carbohydrate

Sicilian Chicken

1 tsp	each dried basil and oregano	5 mL
1/4 tsp	each salt and pepper	1 mL
4	boneless skinless chicken breasts	4
1 tbsp	olive oil	15 mL
1	onion, chopped	1
1	clove garlic, minced	1
1	can (19 oz/540 mL) stewed tomatoes	1
2 tsp	chopped capers or green olives	10 mL
2 tsp	red wine vinegar	10 mL
1/2 tsp	cinnamon	2 mL
	Chopped fresh parsley	

● Combine basil, oregano, salt and pepper; sprinkle half over both sides of chicken. In large nonstick skillet, heat half of the oil over medium-high heat; brown chicken all over, about 4 minutes. Transfer to plate.

● In skillet, heat remaining oil over medium heat; cook onion, garlic and remaining basil mixture, stirring occasionally, for about 5 minutes or until onion is softened.

● Add tomatoes, breaking up with spoon. Add capers, vinegar and cinnamon; bring to boil.

● Return chicken and any accumulated juices to pan; reduce heat, cover and simmer for 10 minutes or until chicken is no longer pink inside. Serve sprinkled with parsley. Makes 4 servings.

Herbs, capers and a touch of cinnamon highlight the tomato sauce in which these chicken breasts simmer. Serve with a short pasta such as fusilli or conchiglie to catch the sauce.

Per serving: about
• 212 calories   • 29 g protein
• 5 g fat   • 13 g carbohydrate
• good source of iron

BONING CHICKEN BREASTS

● Although chicken breasts are much cheaper with skin on and bone in, boneless skinless breasts are a popular choice for their convenience.

When you want to skin and bone your own (and maybe save the bones to make a good stock), here's how.

● First, simply pull off the skin with your fingers and discard. Then, using the tip of a sharp knife, make a shallow cut along the ridge of breastbone

between meat and bone. With short strokes angled to the bone, gradually ease the breast meat from the rib cage. Trim edges neatly.

Chicken with Mushrooms

Familiar white agaracus, or button, mushrooms are most affordable for this dish. But why not try some of the other, more flavorful exotics — big husky portobello, delicate oyster and sturdy shiitake — to make up the pound of mushrooms.

Per serving: about
- 250 calories
- 29 g protein
- 9 g fat
- 13 g carbohydrate
- good source of iron

4	chicken legs, skinned	4
1/4 cup	all-purpose flour	50 mL
3/4 tsp	dried thyme	4 mL
1/4 tsp	pepper	1 mL
1 tbsp	vegetable oil	15 mL
1	onion, chopped	1
6 cups	thickly sliced mushrooms (1 lb/500 g)	1.5 L
1/2 cup	apple juice	125 mL
1 tbsp	balsamic or cider vinegar	15 mL
1/4 tsp	salt	1 mL
	Chopped fresh parsley	

● Separate chicken legs at joint. In plastic bag, combine flour, thyme and pepper; add chicken, in batches if necessary, and shake to coat well.

● In skillet, heat oil over medium-high heat; brown chicken legs all over, about 10 minutes. Transfer to plate.

● Reduce heat to medium. Add onion; cook, stirring occasionally, for about 5 minutes or until softened. Add mushrooms; cook, stirring occasionally, for about 10 minutes or until tender.

● Stir in apple juice and vinegar, scraping up any brown bits from bottom of pan; bring to boil. Return chicken and any accumulated juices to pan; bring to boil. Reduce heat, cover and simmer for 15 minutes.

● Uncover and cook for about 5 minutes or until juices run clear when chicken is pierced. Season with salt. Serve sprinkled with parsley. Makes 4 servings.

Chicken in Tomato Zucchini Sauce

This skillet supper is ideal for families who like spaghetti but are ready to enliven their taste buds. Serve with pasta that cooks at the same time as the chicken.

Per serving: about
- 255 calories
- 30 g protein
- 8 g fat
- 18 g carbohydrate
- high source of fiber
- excellent source of iron

4	chicken legs, skinned	4
2 tsp	vegetable oil	10 mL
2	carrots, thinly sliced	2
1	onion, chopped	1
1	clove garlic, minced	1
1 cup	sliced mushrooms	250 mL
3 tbsp	chopped fresh basil (or 1 tbsp/15 mL dried)	50 mL
1/2 tsp	each salt and pepper	2 mL
1	can (28 oz/796 mL) tomatoes	1
1-1/2 cups	chopped zucchini	375 mL

● Separate chicken legs at joint. In large nonstick skillet, heat oil over medium-high heat; brown chicken all over, about 10 minutes. Transfer to plate.

● Reduce heat to medium. Add carrots, onion and garlic; cook, stirring often, for about 5 minutes or until slightly softened. Add mushrooms, basil, salt and pepper; cook for 5 to 7 minutes or until vegetables are softened and slightly browned.

● Stir in tomatoes, breaking up with spoon; bring to boil. Return chicken and any accumulated juices to pan; bring to boil. Reduce heat, cover and simmer for 15 minutes.

● Add zucchini; simmer for 15 to 20 minutes or until juices run clear when chicken is pierced. Makes 4 servings.

Chili Cornmeal Chicken

3 tbsp	cornmeal	50 mL
1 tbsp	all-purpose flour	15 mL
1 tbsp	chili powder	15 mL
1 tsp	each ground cumin and dried oregano	5 mL
1/4 tsp	salt	1 mL
Pinch	cayenne pepper	Pinch
4	boneless skinless chicken breasts	4
1 tbsp	vegetable oil	15 mL

● In shallow dish, combine cornmeal, flour, chili powder, cumin, oregano, salt and cayenne. Dip each chicken breast into mixture, turning and pressing to coat evenly.

● In nonstick skillet, heat oil over medium heat; cook chicken, turning once, for 10 to 15 minutes or until no longer pink inside. Makes 4 servings.

In the summer and early fall, slice tomatoes and steam green beans and new potatoes to go alongside these crunchy Texan-tasting chicken breasts.

Per serving: about
• 180 calories   • 28 g protein
• 5 g fat   • 3 g carbohydrate

Perfect Chicken Burgers

1	egg	1
1/4 cup	freshly grated Parmesan cheese	50 mL
1/4 cup	dry bread crumbs	50 mL
1	small onion, grated	1
2 tbsp	water	25 mL
2 tsp	Dijon mustard	10 mL
1/4 tsp	salt	1 mL
1	clove garlic, minced	1
1 lb	ground chicken	500 g

● In bowl, beat egg; mix in Parmesan, bread crumbs, onion, water, mustard, salt and garlic. Mix in chicken. Shape into four 3/4-inch (2 cm) thick patties.

● Place patties on greased grill over medium heat; close lid and cook, turning once, for 12 to 14 minutes or until no longer pink inside. Makes 4 servings.

TIP: You can substitute ground turkey, even lean ground beef, for the chicken.

Seasonings should accent the main ingredients, not overwhelm them. See how a touch of mustard and a sprinkle of real Parmesan (Parmigiano Reggiano) in this recipe complement the chicken.

Per serving: about
• 280 calories   • 27 g protein
• 15 g fat   • 7 g carbohydrate

TAKING THE EDGE OFF ANXIOUS APPETITES

● When everyone is impatient to eat, fix a salad. It can be as simple as sliced tomatoes and cucumbers or a tasty assortment of greens (see p. 86), or as fancy as a Caesar or Greek when you have time. Sit down to enjoy every bite while the rest of the meal simmers, grills or bakes.

● Ready-to-dress greens — whether they're a prewashed mix from the produce section or greens you've washed, dried and wrapped in paper towels before refrigerating in plastic bags — make easy-on-the-cook planning more feasible.
● Another healthy munchie kids like before supper is carrot and celery sticks with a

dip. A light dressing is perfect with these vegetables, or with cherry tomatoes, cauliflower and broccoli florets, or sticks cut from broccoli stalks and rutabaga.
● The French do it — why not us? When serving a vegetable, they don't just plop it on a plate with the main course. They serve it alone and first. That way, the

cook doesn't have to juggle three or four items at the same time, and more important, everyone can really savor the tasty asparagus, green beans, sugar snap peas or leeks. Vegetables served this way are fuss-free — usually just steamed or boiled, then drizzled with melted butter, olive oil or a light vinaigrette.

Lemon Chicken

Take advantage of having the barbecue or oven on, and make up supper one night with enough chicken left over for supper another night (see p. 74).

Per serving: about
- 310 calories
- 37 g protein
- 16 g fat
- 1 g carbohydrate

1/4 cup	olive oil	50 mL
1 tbsp	grated lemon rind	15 mL
1/4 cup	lemon juice	50 mL
2	cloves garlic, minced	2
2 tbsp	chopped fresh coriander	25 mL
1 tbsp	minced gingerroot	15 mL
1 tsp	ground cumin	5 mL
1/2 tsp	each salt and pepper	2 mL
8	chicken breasts (about 4 lb/2 kg total)	8

● In large shallow dish, combine oil, lemon rind and juice, garlic, coriander, ginger, cumin, salt and pepper. Add chicken, turning to coat well. Cover and refrigerate, turning occasionally, for at least 2 hours or for up to 4 hours.

● Reserving any marinade, place chicken, skin side down, on greased grill over medium heat; close lid and cook, basting occasionally with any marinade, for 20 minutes. Turn and grill for 8 to 10 minutes longer or just until no longer pink inside. (Or roast in 375°F/190°C oven for about 25 minutes.) Makes 8 servings.

Sausage and Chicken Skewers

These colorful skewers benefit from marinating, but can also be assembled, brushed with herb mixture and grilled right away. If your spice shelf doesn't have herbes de Provence, substitute a mix of 1/4 tsp (1 mL) each of dried thyme, dried basil and crushed fennel seeds.

Per serving: about
- 300 calories
- 26 g protein
- 20 g fat
- 4 g carbohydrate

3	hot or mild Italian sausages (about 1-1/2 lb/750 g total)	3
4	boneless skinless chicken breasts	4
1	each large sweet red and yellow pepper	1
8	bay leaves	8
1/4 cup	red wine vinegar	50 mL
2 tbsp	Dijon mustard	25 mL
1/2 tsp	herbes de Provence or fines herbes	2 mL
2	cloves garlic, minced	2
Pinch	each salt and pepper	Pinch
1/4 cup	olive oil	50 mL

● Prick sausages all over. Place in large skillet; pour in enough water to cover. Bring to boil; reduce heat to low and simmer for about 15 minutes or until firm. Drain and let cool. Cut into 1-inch (2.5 cm) pieces; transfer to large shallow dish.

● Cut chicken into 1-inch (2.5 cm) pieces; add to dish. Core, seed and cut red and yellow peppers; cut into 1-inch (2.5 cm) pieces. Add to dish along with bay leaves.

● In small bowl, whisk together vinegar, mustard, herbes de Provence, garlic, salt and pepper; gradually whisk in oil. Pour over chicken mixture, tossing gently to coat. Cover and refrigerate for at least 4 hours or for up to 8 hours.

● Reserving marinade, alternately thread sweet peppers, sausage, chicken and bay leaves onto eight 12-inch (30 cm) metal skewers.

● Place on greased grill over medium heat; close lid and cook, basting with reserved marinade and turning occasionally, for about 12 minutes or just until chicken is no longer pink inside. Discard bay leaves. Makes 8 servings.

Chicken with Sage, Tomatoes and Lemon ▲

4	chicken breasts	4
3 tbsp	olive oil	50 mL
3/4 tsp	salt	4 mL
1/2 tsp	pepper	2 mL
1	onion, chopped	1
2	cloves garlic, minced	2
1	large carrot, chopped	1
1 tbsp	finely grated lemon rind	15 mL
1 tbsp	chopped fresh sage (or 1 tsp/5 mL dried, crumbled)	15 mL
1	large tomato, peeled, seeded and chopped	1
1/3 cup	chicken stock	75 mL
3 tbsp	lemon juice	50 mL
	Fresh sage leaves	
	Lemon slices	

● Remove skin from chicken; bone, if desired (see p. 13). Sprinkle with pinch each of salt and pepper. In large skillet, heat oil over medium heat; brown chicken lightly on both sides for 5 to 7 minutes. Transfer to plate.

● Add onion, garlic and carrot to pan; cook, stirring often, for about 5 minutes or until onion starts to turn golden. Stir in lemon rind, sage and remaining salt and pepper; cook for 1 minute.

● Add tomato and chicken stock, scraping up brown bits from bottom of pan; bring to boil. Return chicken and any accumulated juices to pan; reduce heat, cover and simmer for 15 minutes, turning chicken once.

● Stir in lemon juice; cook, uncovered, for 5 to 10 minutes or until chicken is no longer pink inside. Serve with pan juices. Garnish with sage leaves and lemon slices. Makes 4 servings.

Associate Food Editor Daphna Rabinovitch likes to pair fresh or dried crumbled sage with chicken not in the traditional stuffing, but in this saucy country-style dish, which she serves with fluffy rice and lightly sautéed zucchini.

Per serving: about
• 260 calories
• 12 g fat
• 29 g protein
• 9 g carbohydrate

Bruschetta Turkey Burgers ◄

1	egg	1
1/4 cup	each dry bread crumbs and grated onion	50 mL
1	clove garlic, minced	1
1 tsp	dried basil	5 mL
1/2 tsp	salt	2 mL
1/4 tsp	pepper	1 mL
1 lb	ground turkey	500 g
4	crusty rolls	4
1	clove garlic	1
4 tsp	freshly grated Parmesan cheese	20 mL
	BRUSCHETTA TOPPING	
1	tomato, chopped	1
1	clove garlic, minced	1
1 tbsp	red wine vinegar	15 mL
1/4 tsp	dried basil	1 mL
Pinch	each salt and pepper	Pinch

● In bowl, beat egg; mix in bread crumbs, onion, 1 tbsp (15 mL) water, minced garlic, basil, salt and pepper. Mix in turkey. Shape into four 1/2-inch (1 cm) thick patties.

● Place patties on greased grill over medium-high heat, or on broiler pan; close lid and cook, turning once, for 12 to 16 minutes or until no longer pink inside.

● BRUSCHETTA TOPPING: Meanwhile, in bowl, combine tomato, garlic, vinegar, basil, salt and pepper.

● Slice rolls in half. Cut garlic clove in half; rub over cut sides of rolls. Grill or broil rolls for 2 minutes or until golden. Top half of each roll with burger and bruschetta; sprinkle with Parmesan. Top with remaining half of roll. Makes 4 servings.

Bruschetta started out as toasted bread, developed into a zingy tomato-and-basil topping for toasted bread and here is deliciously transformed into turkey burgers served on a garlicky toasted bun and topped with chopped fresh tomatoes.

Per serving: about
- 485 calories
- 31 g protein
- 19 g fat
- 46 g carbohydrate
- excellent source of iron

Turkey Potato Patties

1	egg	1
1-1/2 cups	mashed cooked potatoes	375 mL
1 cup	finely chopped cooked turkey	250 mL
1/3 cup	chopped green onion	75 mL
2 tbsp	light mayonnaise	25 mL
1 tsp	Dijon mustard	5 mL
3/4 tsp	salt	4 mL
1/2 tsp	Worcestershire sauce	2 mL
Pinch	pepper	Pinch
2 tsp	butter	10 mL

● In bowl, lightly beat egg; mix in potatoes, turkey and green onion. Stir in mayonnaise, mustard, salt, Worcestershire sauce and pepper. Shape into four 1/2-inch (1 cm) thick patties.

● In nonstick skillet, melt butter over medium heat; cook patties for about 10 minutes or until browned, turning carefully with spatula halfway through. Makes 4 servings.

Match leftover holiday turkey with mashed potatoes and seasonings, shape it into patties, then crisp and brown. Serve with chutney, salsa or chili sauce.

Per serving: about
- 185 calories
- 14 g protein
- 8 g fat
- 15 g carbohydrate

THERE'S MORE TO TURKEY THAN A ROAST

A roast turkey is one grand way to entertain a crowd, and leftovers are favorite fixings for quick-supper sandwiches, soups, casseroles, even patties (see above). But more and more popular because of their versatility are the many new turkey products — smoked turkey breasts and legs, which are ideal substitutes for smoked ham; ground turkey, an excellent alternative to ground chicken or beef; and boned turkey breasts (singles, doubles or in slices) which you can do up in countless ways.

Easy Beef, Pork and Lamb

With these fast-fixing recipes for ground beef, stir-fry steaks and pork and lamb chops, you have the basis for dozens of quick and delicious weekday meals — just add the grain or starch side dish of your choice plus a healthy helping of vegetables or greens.

Stir-Fried Beef and Greens ▶

Stir-fry strips are a super buy for busy cooks. Or look for an inside round steak, often labeled "fast-fry," and slice thinly across the grain. In the Test Kitchen, we use tender sirloin steak or sirloin tip steak for this satisfying dish.

Per serving: about
- 270 calories
- 30 g protein
- 10 g fat
- 15 g carbohydrate

1	each sweet red and yellow pepper	1
1	pkg (10 oz/284 g) fresh spinach	1
1/4 cup	chicken stock	50 mL
3 tbsp	soy sauce	50 mL
1 tbsp	cornstarch	15 mL
1 tbsp	sesame oil	15 mL
1 tbsp	rice or cider vinegar	15 mL
2 tsp	granulated sugar	10 mL
1/4 tsp	hot pepper sauce	1 mL
1 tbsp	vegetable oil	15 mL
1 lb	beef stir-fry strips	500 g
1	large onion, thinly sliced	1
2	cloves garlic, minced	2
1 tbsp	minced gingerroot	15 mL

● Seed, core and cut red and yellow peppers into 1-inch (2.5 cm) squares. Trim and roughly tear spinach. Set aside.

● In small bowl, whisk together stock, soy sauce, cornstarch, sesame oil, vinegar, sugar and hot pepper sauce. Set aside.

● In wok or large nonstick skillet, heat 1 tsp (5 mL) of the oil over high heat; stir-fry half of the beef for 2 minutes or until browned. Transfer to plate. Add another 1 tsp (5 mL) of the oil to wok; stir-fry remaining beef and add to plate.

● Add remaining oil to wok; stir-fry onion, garlic, ginger and red and yellow peppers, adding 1 tbsp (15 mL) water if necessary to prevent sticking, for about 5 minutes or until onion is softened.

● Return beef and any accumulated juices to wok. Add stock mixture and spinach; cook, stirring, for 1 minute or until sauce is slightly thickened and spinach is just wilted. Makes 4 servings.

TIPS
● It is easier to slice meat thinly if it is chilled.
● Browning meat in small batches helps keep the skillet or wok hot, ensuring a delicious flavor base for the whole dish. Be sure to use a large heavy skillet or wok set directly over high heat.

Hamburger Fajitas

*T*ortillas are the wrappers
for this snappy mix of beef,
vegetables and salsa. Just
be sure to wrap the fajita
well in foil so you can munch
from the top down.

Per serving: about
- 545 calories
- 25 g fat
- good source of calcium
- 31 g protein
- 49 g carbohydrate
- excellent source of iron

1 lb	lean ground beef	500 g
1	onion, cut in strips	1
2	cloves garlic, minced	2
1 tsp	chili powder	5 mL
1/4 tsp	each salt and pepper	1 mL
1/2 cup	salsa	125 mL
1	each sweet red and green pepper, chopped	1
1	small zucchini, thinly sliced	1
4	10-inch (25 cm) flour tortillas	4
2/3 cup	low-fat sour cream	150 mL
2 tsp	Dijon mustard	10 mL
2 tbsp	chopped fresh coriander	25 mL

● In large nonstick skillet, cook beef over medium-high heat, breaking up with back of spoon, until no longer pink. Drain off any fat. Reduce heat to medium. Add onion, garlic, chili powder, salt and pepper; cook, stirring often, for 5 minutes or until onion is softened.

● Add salsa, red and green peppers and zucchini; cook, stirring, for about 5 minutes or until tender-crisp and mixture is moist but no longer watery.

● Meanwhile, wrap tortillas in foil; heat in 350°F (180°C) oven for 5 minutes or until warmed through.

● Stir sour cream with mustard. Spread evenly over tortillas; top with beef mixture and coriander and roll up. Makes 4 servings.

TIP: Fresh coriander is a wonderful addition to your herb garden or crisper. When it's unavailable, substitute an equal amount of chopped fresh parsley and 1 tsp (5 mL) dried coriander, or cilantro, as this herb is known in Spanish.

Potato Beef Skillet Supper

*Y*ou don't have to wait for
leftover roast beef to make a
memorable skillet hash. One
of the tricks is to use a can of
seasoned stewed tomatoes.
Here it's pasta-style, but you
can substitute regular canned
tomatoes, with a pinch of
oregano and basil.

Per serving: about
- 355 calories
- 15 g fat
- good source of calcium
- 29 g protein
- 25 g carbohydrate
- excellent source of iron

1 tsp	vegetable oil	5 mL
2	potatoes, peeled and cubed	2
1	onion, chopped	1
1	clove garlic, minced	1
1 tsp	each dried oregano and basil	5 mL
1 lb	lean ground beef	500 g
3/4 cup	shredded part-skim mozzarella cheese	175 mL
1/2 tsp	salt	2 mL
1/4 tsp	pepper	1 mL
2 cups	canned pasta-style stewed tomatoes	500 mL

● In large nonstick skillet, heat oil over medium-high heat; cook potatoes, stirring often, for about 7 minutes or until browned. Transfer to plate.

● Add onion, garlic, oregano and basil to skillet. Add beef; cook, breaking up with back of spoon, for about 5 minutes or until beef is no longer pink.

● Push mixture to side of skillet; spoon off fat. Spread beef mixture evenly over bottom of skillet; arrange potatoes evenly over top.

● Sprinkle with 1/2 cup (125 mL) of the mozzarella; season with salt and pepper. Spread tomatoes over top; sprinkle with remaining cheese. Reduce heat to medium; cover and cook for 15 minutes or until potatoes are tender. Makes 4 servings.

Swedish Meatballs in Mushroom Sauce ▲

2 tsp	vegetable oil	10 mL
6 cups	sliced mushrooms (1 lb/500 g)	1.5 L
2 tsp	chopped fresh dill (or 1/2 tsp/2 mL dried dillweed)	10 mL
1/4 tsp	each salt and pepper	1 mL
2/3 cup	2% evaporated milk	150 mL
3 tbsp	rye cracker crumbs	50 mL
3 tbsp	finely chopped onion	50 mL
1/2 tsp	ground allspice	2 mL
1/4 tsp	nutmeg	1 mL
3/4 lb	lean ground beef	375 g
4 tsp	all-purpose flour	20 mL
2/3 cup	beef stock	150 mL

● In large nonstick skillet, heat oil over medium-high heat; cook mushrooms, dill and pinch each of the salt and pepper, stirring occasionally, for 10 minutes or until just starting to brown and liquid is evaporated. Transfer to bowl.

● Meanwhile, in separate bowl, combine 2 tbsp (25 mL) of the milk, the cracker crumbs, onion, allspice, nutmeg and remaining salt and pepper. Mix in beef. Shape into 1-inch (2.5 cm) balls. Add to skillet; cook, turning often, for 8 minutes or until browned.

● Return mushrooms to skillet; sprinkle with flour and stir for 30 seconds or until flour is absorbed. Pour in stock and remaining milk, scraping up brown bits from bottom of pan; bring to boil. Reduce heat and simmer, stirring occasionally, for 4 minutes or until thickened and meatballs are no longer pink inside. Makes 4 servings.

We've cut back on the fat without sacrificing any creaminess or flavor in this lightened-up family favorite. The secret is using 2% or skim evaporated milk instead of traditional whipping cream — but no one will ever guess!

Per serving: about
- 295 calories
- 17 g fat
- excellent source of iron
- 22 g protein
- 15 g carbohydrate

Roast Beef Hash

Colorful vegetables and a dash of chili give roast beef leftovers the stylish finale they deserve.

Per serving: about
- 435 calories
- 12 g fat
- high source of fiber
- 40 g protein
- 43 g carbohydrate
- excellent source of iron

1	baking potato	1
1/3 cup	beef stock	75 mL
1 tsp	vegetable oil	5 mL
1	small onion, chopped	1
3/4 tsp	chili powder	4 mL
1-1/2 cups	diced cooked beef	375 mL
1	small sweet green pepper, chopped	1
3/4 cup	frozen corn kernels	175 mL
1/4 cup	chili sauce	50 mL
1/4 cup	shredded part-skim mozzarella, Monterey Jack or Danbo cheese	50 mL

● Peel potato and cut into 1/2-inch (1 cm) cubes. In nonstick skillet, bring stock and potato to boil; reduce heat, cover and simmer for about 8 minutes or until almost tender and stock is absorbed.

● Push potato to side of pan. Pour oil into other side of pan; heat over medium heat. Add onion and chili powder to oil; cook, stirring often, for about 5 minutes or until onion is softened.

● Increase heat to high. Add beef, green pepper, corn and chili sauce, stirring together with potato and onion; cook, stirring often, for about 5 minutes or just until liquid is evaporated and beef is heated through. Remove from heat.

● Sprinkle with cheese; let stand for about 2 minutes or until melted. Makes 2 servings.

Hoisin Meat Loaf Muffins

These gingery, muffin-size meat loaves bake in half the time of a regular meat loaf. Use the baking time to prepare quick-cooking vegetables such as green beans, broccoli, broccoflower, Swiss chard or spinach — or slice a plateful of tomatoes and warm up crusty rolls.

Per serving: about
- 295 calories
- 15 g fat
- good source of iron
- 25 g protein
- 13 g carbohydrate

1	egg	1
3	green onions, chopped	3
1	clove garlic, minced	1
1/3 cup	dry bread crumbs	75 mL
2 tbsp	hoisin sauce	25 mL
1 tbsp	soy sauce	15 mL
1 tbsp	minced gingerroot (or 1/2 tsp/2 mL ground ginger)	15 mL
1 tbsp	Dijon mustard	15 mL
1/4 tsp	salt	1 mL
1 lb	lean ground beef	500 g
	GLAZE	
1-1/2 tsp	hoisin sauce	7 mL
1-1/2 tsp	soy sauce	7 mL

● In large bowl, lightly beat egg; mix in green onions, garlic, bread crumbs, hoisin sauce, soy sauce, ginger, mustard and salt. Mix in beef. Divide evenly into eight portions; lightly press each into ungreased muffin cup.

● GLAZE: Whisk together hoisin and soy sauces; brush over meat mixture.

● Bake in 400°F (200°C) oven for 20 to 25 minutes or until no longer pink inside. Drain off fat. Makes 4 servings.

Pepper Beef Kabobs ▲

1 lb	sirloin tip steak, 1 inch (2.5 cm) thick	500 g
	PEPPER MARINADE	
2 tbsp	vegetable oil	25 mL
4 tsp	balsamic or red wine vinegar	20 mL
2 tsp	dry mustard	10 mL
2 tsp	coarsely ground or cracked pepper	10 mL
Pinch	cayenne pepper	Pinch

● Cut steak into 1-inch (2.5 cm) cubes; place in bowl.

● PEPPER MARINADE: Combine oil, vinegar, mustard and ground and cayenne peppers; add to bowl, stirring to coat beef. Cover and marinate in refrigerator for at least 1 hour or for up to 12 hours.

● Thread beef onto metal skewers. Place on greased grill over medium-high heat; close lid and cook, turning 3 times, for 10 minutes or until browned yet still pink inside. Makes 4 servings.

Cube and season a thick sirloin or inside round steak before you sizzle it on the grill. Here, it's presented in all its glory with couscous, vibrant vegetables and a garnish of greens.

Per serving: about
- 205 calories
- 24 g protein
- 11 g fat
- 1 g carbohydrate
- good source of iron

Down-Under Marinated Steak

This tangy marinade, just right with steaks, is the creation of Gillian and Rob Hogarth, who welcome visitors from around the world to Robsley, their Queensland, Australia, ranch. They serve the steak with baked potatoes and lots of sliced onions that cook in a cast-iron skillet until golden and tender.

Per serving: about
- 195 calories
- 22 g protein
- 5 g fat
- 15 g carbohydrate
- good source of iron

1/2 cup	packed brown sugar	125 mL
1/2 cup	tomato sauce	125 mL
1/4 cup	Worcestershire sauce	50 mL
1/4 cup	vinegar	50 mL
1/4 tsp	pepper	1 mL
2 lb	sirloin steak, about 1 inch (2.5 cm) thick	1 kg
	Salt	

● In shallow glass dish, stir together sugar, tomato and Worcestershire sauces, vinegar and pepper. Add steak, turning to coat. Cover and marinate in refrigerator for at least 1 hour or for up to 4 hours, turning 3 or 4 times.

● Reserving marinade in saucepan, place steak on greased grill over medium-high heat; close lid and cook, turning once, for 16 to 20 minutes for rare or to desired doneness.

● Transfer to cutting board; tent with foil and let stand for 5 minutes. Season with salt to taste. Slice thinly across the grain.

● Meanwhile, bring marinade to boil; boil for 3 minutes, stirring. Serve with steak. Makes 8 servings.

Greek Grilled Steak

It takes only minutes in the morning to put together the marinade for this steak. Later in the day, it's ready for grilling, with the bonus of having enough for two meals — hot the first supper, cold in a salad (see p. 75) the next.

Per serving: about
- 225 calories
- 34 g protein
- 9 g fat
- 1 g carbohydrate
- good source of iron

3 lb	inside round steak, 1-1/2 inches (4 cm) thick	1.5 kg
3 tbsp	red wine vinegar	50 mL
3 tbsp	olive oil	50 mL
2	cloves garlic, minced	2
2 tbsp	each chopped fresh oregano and mint (or 2 tsp/10 mL dried)	25 mL
1/4 tsp	pepper	1 mL

● Place steak in shallow glass dish. Whisk together vinegar, oil, garlic, oregano, mint and pepper; pour over steak, turning to coat. Cover and marinate in refrigerator for at least 8 hours or for up to 24 hours, turning occasionally.

● Reserving marinade, place steak on greased grill over medium-high heat; close lid and cook, basting occasionally with marinade, for 20 to 30 minutes or until rare.

● Transfer to cutting board; tent with foil and let stand for 10 minutes before slicing thinly across the grain. Makes 8 servings.

Rib Eye with Herb Jus

8 oz	rib eye steak	250 g
1 tsp	olive oil	5 mL
Pinch	salt	Pinch
1	clove garlic, minced	1
1/4 cup	beef stock	50 mL
1-1/2 tsp	chopped fresh sage	7 mL
1 tsp	red wine vinegar	5 mL
1/2 tsp	Dijon mustard	2 mL
Pinch	each pepper and granulated sugar	Pinch

● Trim fat from steak. In heavy or nonstick skillet, heat oil over medium-high heat; cook steak, turning once, for 6 minutes or until medium-rare. Transfer to heated plate. Sprinkle with salt; tent with foil and let stand for 5 minutes.

● Meanwhile, add garlic to pan; cook, stirring, for 30 seconds. Add 2 tbsp (25 mL) water, beef stock, sage, vinegar, mustard, pepper and sugar; bring to boil, scraping up brown bits from bottom. Boil for 2 minutes or until slightly reduced. Add any juices accumulated on plate.

● To serve, cut steak in half or thinly slice steak on the diagonal. Drizzle with sauce. Makes 2 servings.

Slicing the steak across the grain makes this satisfying serving look even more generous.

Per serving: about
- 250 calories
- 16 g fat
- 24 g protein
- 1 g carbohydrate

TIP: If you can't find fresh sage, substitute 1-1/2 tsp (7 mL) chopped fresh parsley and 1/4 tsp (1 mL) crumbled dried sage.

KEEPING YOUR FREEZER STOCKED

Buying fresh meat and poultry once every week or so and freezing it for suppers until the next time you shop is a convenience Canadians really enjoy. Although fresh products are unbeatable, quick freezing and slow thawing in the refrigerator can give you safe, delicious-tasting food for your money.

1 If buying in bulk, divide meat, poultry or fish as soon as you get home into amounts that are convenient for your recipes and household.

2 Wrap products in freezer paper or put in freezer bags. Enclose already packaged and portioned meats, poultry or fish in freezer bags, pressing out air before sealing and freezing.

3 Mark quantity and date of purchase on each package.

4 If you are going to freeze fresh meat, poultry or fish, consider bulk-size containers of flash-frozen products. Unseasoned and uncoated fillets, chops and chicken parts allow you the most flexibility when choosing recipes.

5 Always thaw frozen meat, poultry and fish in the refrigerator, allowing 5 hours per lb (500 g); never leave them on the counter at room temperature.

6 Get into the habit of transferring frozen meat or poultry from freezer to fridge the day before you need it. Thaw on a plate to prevent juices from dripping onto other foods.

Grilled Mustard-Sage Pork and Zucchini ▶

Today's lean pork is perfect for quick cooking over the coals and for showcasing bold-flavored glazes. You can replace 1 tsp (5 mL) crumbled dried sage for fresh.

Per serving: about
- 235 calories
- 24 g protein
- 10 g fat
- 14 g carbohydrate

1/4 cup	Dijon mustard	50 mL
2 tbsp	liquid honey	25 mL
1 tbsp	finely chopped fresh sage	15 mL
1/2 tsp	salt	2 mL
1/4 tsp	pepper	1 mL
2 tsp	butter, melted	10 mL
1 tsp	grated lemon rind	5 mL
2	butterflied boneless pork loin chops, 1 inch (2.5 cm) thick (1 lb/500 g)	2
4	small zucchini	4

● In small bowl, stir together mustard, honey, sage, salt and pepper. Spoon half into separate bowl; stir in butter and lemon rind. Set aside for zucchini.

● Brush pork with 2 tbsp (25 mL) of the mustard, honey and sage mixture. Place on greased grill over medium-high heat; close lid and cook, turning once and brushing with the rest of mustard mixture, for 14 minutes or until juices run clear when pork is pierced but hint of pink remains inside. Transfer to plate; tent with foil and keep warm.

● Meanwhile, slice zucchini lengthwise into 1/4-inch (5 mm) thick strips; brush with reserved mustard, lemon and butter mixture to coat. Add to grill; cook, turning once, for about 8 minutes or until tender-crisp. Cut each pair of pork chops in half; serve with zucchini. Makes 4 servings.

TIP: Any lean meat will toughen if overcooked. This is especially important to remember with pork, since the advice always was to cook it to well-done to avoid any chance of trichinosis. Now there's a simple way to test pork. Just slit the meat with the tip of a sharp, pointed knife. When the pink inside has started to disappear and the juices run clear, it's ready.

BLT on the Barbecue

In summer, mate robust ripe tomatoes, back bacon and the grill for a twist on a favorite sandwich. Other times of the year, opt for Canadian hot-house tomatoes (always tastier than imports) and the broiler to crisp the bacon and toast the buns.

Per serving: about
- 400 calories
- 25 g protein
- 11 g fat
- 51 g carbohydrate
- good source of iron

1	piece back bacon, 12 oz (375 g)	1
2 tbsp	liquid honey	25 mL
1 tsp	Worcestershire sauce	5 mL
4	onion buns	4
2 tbsp	light mayonnaise	25 mL
1 tbsp	grainy mustard	15 mL
4	lettuce leaves	4
2	tomatoes, sliced	2
Pinch	pepper	Pinch

● Cut bacon into 1/4-inch (5 mm) thick slices. In small bowl, combine honey and Worcestershire sauce. Place bacon on greased grill over medium-high heat; brush with half of the honey mixture. Cook, turning once and brushing with remaining honey mixture, for 5 minutes for precooked bacon, 7 minutes for uncooked, or until cooked through and well marked.

● Meanwhile, cut buns in half. Toast, cut side down, on grill. Combine mayonnaise and mustard; spread evenly over bottom halves. Top each with 1 lettuce leaf and some of the tomato slices; season with pepper. Top with bacon and remaining tomatoes and bun halves. Makes 4 servings.

VARIATION
● MLT ON THE BARBECUE: Replace honey and Worcestershire sauce with 2 tbsp (25 mL) balsamic or red wine vinegar, 1 tbsp (15 mL) chopped fresh oregano and pinch salt. Substitute 4 portobello mushroom caps for bacon. Place on greased grill over medium heat; close lid and cook, turning and basting occasionally, for about 12 minutes or until tender.

Ginger-Orange Pork Chops

Thick pork chops will turn out juicier on the grill than thin ones. If your meat counter carries only 1/2-inch (1 cm) thick pork chops, decrease the cooking time by about 1 minute on each side. Use bone-in chops if they're easier to find.

Per serving: about
• 275 calories • 38 g protein
• 11 g fat • 3 g carbohydrate

4	boneless pork loin chops (1 lb/500 g)	4
1 tsp	grated orange rind	5 mL
1/3 cup	orange juice	75 mL
2 tsp	minced gingerroot	10 mL
1	clove garlic, minced	1
1	green onion, finely chopped	1
Pinch	cinnamon	Pinch
	Salt and pepper	

● Trim any fat from pork; slash edges at 1-inch (2.5 cm) intervals. Arrange in single layer in shallow dish.

● Combine orange rind and juice, ginger, garlic, green onion and cinnamon; pour over chops, turning to coat well. Cover and marinate at room temperature for 30 minutes or in refrigerator for up to 24 hours, turning occasionally.

● Reserving marinade, place chops on greased grill over medium-high heat; close lid and cook, turning once and basting occasionally with marinade, for about 10 minutes or until juices run clear when pork is pierced and hint of pink remains inside. Season with salt and pepper to taste. Makes 4 servings.

TIP: When cold and snow make outdoor barbecuing just a delicious memory, carry on inside with a cast-iron ridged grill pan, now available in kitchen shops and hardware stores. This inexpensive pan works surprisingly well for chops, chicken breasts, steaks, burgers and firm fish. Of course, you can also broil for healthy, fast meals.

Stove-Top Barbecued Pork Chops

Keep summer sizzling year-round with chops done up in this tangy sauce. Baked potatoes and carrot coins are a good match for the sweet-and-sour flavors of the meat.

Per serving: about
• 210 calories • 23 g protein
• 8 g fat • 11 g carbohydrate

4	boneless pork loin chops (1 lb/500 g)	4
2 tsp	vegetable oil	10 mL
1	onion, chopped	1
1/3 cup	ketchup	75 mL
1 tbsp	cider vinegar	15 mL
1 tbsp	Worcestershire sauce	15 mL
2 tsp	packed brown sugar	10 mL
1/4 tsp	each dry mustard and pepper	1 mL

● Trim any fat from pork. In large nonstick skillet, heat oil over medium-high heat; brown chops, turning once, for 6 to 8 minutes. Transfer to plate.

● Add onion to skillet; cook over medium heat, stirring, for 4 minutes or until softened.

● Combine ketchup, vinegar, Worcestershire sauce, sugar, mustard and pepper; pour into skillet and bring to boil.

● Return pork and any accumulated juices to skillet, turning to coat. Reduce heat and simmer, stirring sauce and turning chops occasionally, for about 8 minutes or until juices run clear when pork is pierced and hint of pink remains inside. Add 1 tbsp (15 mL) water to thin sauce, if desired. Makes 4 servings.

5-MINUTE COUSCOUS

Couscous, a traditional staple of North African cooking, has a precooked version that is becoming more available in Canadian bulk-food outlets, supermarkets and health-food stores. It's a boon to busy cooks, since it plumps up and is ready to serve in 5 minutes.

● The simplest way to prepare it is to bring 1-1/2 cups (375 mL) water and a pinch of salt to a boil in a saucepan. Stir in 1 cup (250 mL) couscous. Remove from heat, cover and let stand for 5 minutes. Fluff with a fork. Makes 3 cups (750 mL), enough for 4 servings.

Pork Chops Carbonade

4	boneless pork loin chops (1 lb/500 g)	4
1/2 tsp	salt	2 mL
1/4 tsp	pepper	1 mL
1 tbsp	vegetable oil	15 mL
1	large onion, thinly sliced	1
2 tbsp	cider vinegar	25 mL
1 tbsp	packed brown sugar	15 mL
1 cup	beer	250 mL
1/4 cup	beef stock	50 mL
2 tsp	cornstarch	10 mL

● Trim any fat from pork; sprinkle with salt and pepper. In large skillet, heat oil over medium-high heat; brown chops, turning once, for 6 to 8 minutes. Transfer to plate.

● Reduce heat to medium. Add 2 tbsp (25 mL) water to pan, scraping up any brown bits from bottom. Add onion, vinegar and sugar; cook, stirring occasionally, for about 10 minutes or until softened.

● Add beer and stock; bring to boil. Reduce heat and simmer for 3 to 4 minutes or until reduced by half. Dissolve cornstarch in 1 tbsp (15 mL) water; add to pan and cook, stirring, for 1 minute or until thickened.

● Return chops and any accumulated juices to pan, spooning juices over top; cook for about 3 minutes or until juices run clear when pork is pierced and hint of pink remains inside. Makes 4 servings.

VARIATION

● NO-BEER PORK CHOPS: Substitute 1/3 cup (75 mL) apple juice and 2 tbsp (25 mL) water for beer. Increase stock to 3/4 cup (175 mL). Decrease salt to 1/4 tsp (1 mL).

B*ig on taste and short on time, this skillet dish borrows mellow onions and hearty beer from a Belgian beef stew by the same name. Serve up with lemony green beans and mashed potatoes.*

Per serving: about
- 215 calories
- 9 g fat
- 20 g protein
- 11 g carbohydrate

Pineapple-Glazed Pork Chops

4	boneless pork loin chops (1 lb/500 g)	4
1/4 tsp	each salt and pepper	1 mL
1 tbsp	vegetable oil	15 mL
4	green onions, chopped	4
1	small clove garlic, minced	1
1 tsp	minced gingerroot (or pinch ground ginger)	5 mL
1/2 cup	crushed pineapple	125 mL
1/3 cup	strained apricot jam	75 mL
2 tbsp	soy sauce	25 mL
1 tbsp	rice vinegar or white wine vinegar	15 mL

● Trim any fat from pork; sprinkle with salt and pepper. In large nonstick skillet, heat oil over medium-high heat; cook chops, turning once, for 6 to 8 minutes or until browned. Transfer to plate.

● Reduce heat to medium. Add 2 tbsp (25 mL) water to pan, scraping up any brown bits from bottom. Reserve 1 tbsp (15 mL) green onions; set aside. Add remaining green onions, garlic and ginger to pan; cook, stirring, for about 3 minutes or until onions are softened. Stir in pineapple, apricot jam, soy sauce and vinegar; simmer for about 2 minutes or until slightly thickened.

● Return pork and any accumulated juices to pan; cook, turning to coat, for about 3 minutes or until juices run clear when pork is pierced and hint of pink remains inside. Serve sprinkled with reserved green onions. Makes 4 servings.

S*immer up a bed of parboiled or plain long-grain rice to go with these fruity chops.*

Per serving: about
- 265 calories
- 9 g fat
- 21 g protein
- 26 g carbohydrate

Orange Teriyaki Pork Stir-Fry

When you use frozen prepared stir-fry vegetables, the only knife work required is slicing the pork and mincing the garlic. Serve over rice or precooked Asian noodles.

Per serving: about
- 270 calories
- 26 g protein
- 9 g fat
- 21 g carbohydrate

12 oz	fast-fry boneless pork cutlets	375 g
1-1/2 tsp	grated orange rind	7 mL
1/3 cup	each orange juice and teriyaki sauce	75 mL
1 tbsp	Dijon mustard	15 mL
2 tsp	cornstarch	10 mL
2	cloves garlic, minced	2
2 tsp	grated gingerroot	10 mL
1 tbsp	vegetable oil	15 mL
1	bag (750 g) frozen stir-fry vegetables	1

● Trim any fat from pork; cut across the grain into thin strips.

● Whisk together orange rind and juice, teriyaki sauce, mustard, cornstarch, garlic and ginger; set aside.

● In wok or large nonstick skillet, heat oil over high heat; stir-fry pork for 2 to 3 minutes or until just a hint of pink remains inside. Transfer to plate.

● Add vegetables to wok; cover and cook for 3 minutes or until thawed. Push vegetables up side of wok; cook, uncovered, for 1 minute or until water evaporates.

● Pour orange juice mixture into wok; cook, stirring, for 1 minute or until thickened. Return pork and any accumulated juices to pan; cook, stirring to combine with vegetables, until coated with sauce and steaming. Makes 4 servings.

TIP: If you prefer to put together your own selection of vegetables — broccoli florets, sliced peeled broccoli stems, sweet red or green pepper strips, thinly sliced onion, for example — measure out 3 cups (750 L) of them and add to wok along with 2 tbsp (25 mL) of water after removing the pork. Cover and cook, tossing once, for 3 minutes. There is no need to evaporate juices.

FROZEN AND CANNED VEGETABLES TO THE RESCUE

Professionals call it "prep time" — and that's just what home cooks find lacking on weeknights. When you're rushed, canned and frozen vegetables are worth considering for their price, quality and nutrition. Everything is microwave- or stove-top ready and can be on the table in the time it takes to round up the rest of the meal.

Canned Vegetables
● Corn, tomatoes and beets are very recommendable.
● Cans of potatoes and carrots can be last-minute lifesavers when you're preparing a stew.
● Cans or jars of roasted peppers and artichokes are more exotic, but are handy to have on your pantry shelf when a stir-fry, salad or omelette needs a lift.

Frozen Vegetables
● Frozen vegetables have gone well beyond the peas and carrots of the 1950s. Snow peas, green beans, lima beans, broccoli, cauliflower, spinach, squash, rutabaga (aka turnip), onions, sweet peppers or international mixes of vegetables and flavors provide amazing help to a harried cook.

● Frozen vegetables take well to the microwave, allowing beginner cooks to lend a hand when time is short.
● In our *Canadian Living* kitchens, we prefer unsauced and unseasoned frozen vegetables, because they let you season to taste and are lower in fat, sodium and price than the prepared varieties.

Skillet Pork Chops with Black Beans

4	pork chops (1 lb/500 g)	4
1/4 tsp	each salt and pepper	1 mL
1 tsp	vegetable oil	5 mL
1	small onion, chopped	1
2	cloves garlic, minced	2
1	sweet red pepper, chopped	1
1 tsp	dried oregano	5 mL
1/2 tsp	ground cumin	2 mL
Pinch	cayenne pepper	Pinch
3/4 cup	chicken stock	175 mL
1/4 cup	apple juice	50 mL
1	can (19 oz/540 mL) black or navy (pea) beans, drained and rinsed	1

● Trim fat from pork; sprinkle with salt and pepper. In large nonstick skillet, heat oil over medium-high heat; cook pork, turning once, for about 5 minutes or until browned. Transfer to plate.

● Reduce heat to medium. Add onion, garlic, red pepper, oregano, cumin and cayenne; cook, stirring occasionally, for 5 minutes or until onion is softened.

● Add chicken stock and apple juice; bring to simmer. Return pork and any accumulated juices to skillet; simmer for 5 minutes, turning once.

● Stir in beans; simmer for 3 minutes or until liquid is reduced by half, juices run clear when pork is pierced and just a hint of pink remains inside. Makes 4 servings.

Here's a fresh new look at lean pork cooked with beans and tomatoes. This skillet supper is delicious over pasta, rice or mashed potatoes.

Per serving: about
- 405 calories
- 11 g fat
- 45 g protein
- 28 g carbohydrate

Herbed Pork Cutlets

1 lb	fast-fry boneless pork cutlets	500 g
1	egg	1
1/3 cup	dry bread crumbs	75 mL
1/4 cup	chopped fresh basil	50 mL
2 tbsp	chopped fresh oregano	25 mL
1 tbsp	freshly grated Parmesan cheese	15 mL
1 tsp	chopped fresh thyme	5 mL
1/2 tsp	pepper	2 mL
1/4 tsp	salt	1 mL
2 tbsp	vegetable oil	25 mL

● Trim any fat from pork. In shallow dish, lightly beat egg. In separate shallow dish, stir together bread crumbs, basil, oregano, Parmesan cheese, thyme, pepper and salt.

● Dip pork into egg, turning to coat well; press into bread crumb mixture, turning to coat all over.

● In large skillet, heat half of the oil over medium heat; cook pork, in batches and adding remaining oil if necessary, turning once, for 8 to 10 minutes or until juices run clear when pork is pierced and a hint of pink remains inside. Makes 4 servings.

Call them fast-fry cutlets or call them scaloppine — either way, thin slices of boneless lean pork dazzle in a crisp herb-speckled coating.

Per serving: about
- 255 calories
- 12 g fat
- 28 g protein
- 7 g carbohydrate

TIPS

● If pork cutlets are not available at the meat counter, a very tender substitute is pork tenderloin, sliced thinly on the diagonal.

● You can replace the fresh basil with 1 tbsp (15 mL) dried, and the oregano with 1 tsp (5 mL) dried.

Rosemary Mustard Lamb Chops ▶

Rosemary is the herb of choice for lamb, as this quick-supper grill shows. In a pinch, you can substitute fresh oregano or marjoram.

Per serving: about
- 125 calories
- 5 g fat
- 18 g protein
- trace carbohydrate

8	lamb loin chops (about 1 lb/500 g)	8
2 tbsp	raspberry vinegar	25 mL
1 tbsp	Dijon mustard	15 mL
1 tbsp	soy sauce	15 mL
2 tsp	minced fresh rosemary (or 1/2 tsp/2 mL dried)	10 mL
1 tsp	olive oil	5 mL
1	clove garlic, minced	1

● Trim any fat from lamb; arrange in single layer in large shallow dish. Whisk together vinegar, mustard, soy sauce, rosemary, oil and garlic; pour over chops, turning to coat well. Cover and marinate in refrigerator for at least 2 hours or for up to 8 hours, turning occasionally.

● Discard marinade. Place chops on greased grill over medium-high heat; close lid and cook, turning once, for about 10 minutes for medium-rare or until desired doneness. Transfer to platter; tent with foil and let stand for 5 minutes. Makes 4 servings.

TIPS
● This lamb is an ideal make-ahead dish. In a plastic freezer bag, combine the lamb with the marinade. Seal the bag and freeze for up to 2 weeks, then thaw completely in the refrigerator before grilling.
● To keep lamb or pork chops from curling on the grill, be sure to nick the curved edges, usually at about 1/2-inch (1 cm) intervals.

Thai-Inspired Pork and Vegetable Curry

Thai cooking is influenced by Indian cuisine. Here, fresh basil adds coolness to a mildly spicy curry that's best served over steaming mounds of rice.

Per serving: about
- 310 calories
- 11 g fat
- good source of iron
- 28 g protein
- 26 g carbohydrate

1 lb	lean boneless pork	500 g
1 tbsp	vegetable oil	15 mL
4 tsp	red curry paste (or 1-1/2 tsp/7 mL curry powder)	20 mL
1 cup	sliced green beans	250 mL
1	onion, cut in wedges	1
2 tbsp	fish sauce	25 mL
1 cup	thickly sliced mushrooms	250 mL
1	sweet red pepper, thinly sliced	1
1	can (14 oz/398 mL) corn kernels, drained	1
1/3 cup	chopped fresh basil	75 mL
1 tsp	granulated sugar	5 mL

● Trim any fat from pork; cut across the grain into thin strips. Set aside.

● In wok or large nonstick skillet, heat oil over high heat; stir-fry curry paste for 1 minute. Add pork; stir-fry for 3 minutes or until just a hint of pink remains inside. Transfer to plate.

● Add green beans, onion and fish sauce to pan; stir-fry for 5 minutes. Add mushrooms, red pepper and corn; stir-fry for about 2 minutes or until vegetables are tender.

● Return pork and any accumulated juices to pan. Add basil and sugar; stir-fry for 1 minute or until steaming. Makes 4 servings.

CURRY PASTE
Stores that sell Southeast Asian ingredients — Thai, of course, but also Vietnamese and Chinese — stock small cans of Thai red curry paste. This ready-to-use paste is a fabulous addition to your curry repertoire. Its aromatic blend replaces a number of spices and is vastly superior to any popular brand of curry powder. If you like, you can substitute Indian curry pastes. Lately, supermarkets have begun adding ingredients such as Thai red curry and Indian pastes to their international selections.

Fish is Fabulous!

Mysteriously, fish is one of those items we happily choose in a restaurant but rarely seem to include in menus for weekday dinners at home. We hope the easy and very pleasing recipes we've provided here — plus the fact that fish is fast to make and especially good for you — will inspire you to bake, broil or barbecue it more often.

Fish Baked in Black Bean Sauce ▶

Fermented black beans, now stocked in major supermarkets, add immense taste to any dish. Here, their saltiness is perfectly balanced with honey, lemon, ginger and spinach.

Per serving: about
- 205 calories
- 25 g protein
- 5 g fat
- 13 g carbohydrate
- good source of iron

1	pkg (10 oz/300 g) fresh spinach, chopped	1
1	carrot, grated	1
1 lb	Boston bluefish fillets	500 g
2 tbsp	black bean sauce	25 mL
1 tbsp	liquid honey	15 mL
1 tbsp	lemon juice	15 mL
1 tsp	chopped gingerroot	5 mL
2	green onions, finely chopped	2

● Spread chopped spinach in 8-inch (2 L) square baking dish; sprinkle with carrot. Arrange fish over top.

● Stir together black bean sauce, honey, lemon juice, ginger and green onions; spread evenly over fish. Cover with foil.

● Bake in 425°F (220°C) oven for 10 to 12 minutes or until fish is opaque and flakes easily when tested with fork. Makes 4 servings.

Crispy Baked Fish

You can cook any kind of firm fish fillets this kid-pleasing way. If using a block of frozen fish, place the package in the fridge the night before to thaw, and pat fillets dry before coating.

Per serving: about
- 130 calories
- 16 g protein
- 4 g fat
- 7 g carbohydrate

1	egg	1
1/2 cup	fine dry bread crumbs	125 mL
1/2 tsp	each salt and paprika	2 mL
1/4 tsp	pepper	1 mL
1 lb	fish fillets (cod, sole or haddock)	500 g
1 tbsp	butter, melted	15 mL

● In small bowl, beat egg. In shallow dish, mix together bread crumbs, salt, paprika and pepper. Dip fish into egg, then into bread crumbs, turning to coat.

● Place fish on greased baking sheet; drizzle with butter. Bake in 475°F (240°C) oven for 10 minutes or until fish is opaque and flakes easily when tested with fork. Makes 6 servings.

Fish Fillets Florentine

Here is a winning set of flavors for fish — fillets baked on a bed of spinach (hence the name Florentine) with a creamy light cheese sauce and a crispy topping.

Per serving: about
- 290 calories
- 13 g fat
- excellent source of calcium
- 29 g protein
- 14 g carbohydrate
- good source of iron

1	pkg (10 oz/300 g) frozen spinach, thawed	1
2 tsp	butter	10 mL
1	small onion, chopped	1
8 oz	cod or sole fillets, cut in 2 pieces	250 g
1/3 cup	milk	75 mL
1/4 cup	light cream cheese	50 mL
1 tbsp	each dry bread crumbs and freshly grated Parmesan cheese	15 mL

● In sieve, press moisture out of spinach; chop coarsely. In small skillet, melt butter over medium heat; cook onion, stirring occasionally, for 3 minutes.

● Add spinach to pan; cook, stirring often, for about 4 minutes or until moisture is evaporated. Spread in 8-inch (2 L) square baking or gratin dish. Nestle fish in spinach mixture.

● Meanwhile, in microwave or on stove top, heat milk with cream cheese until smooth; pour over fish mixture. Sprinkle with bread crumbs and Parmesan cheese.

● Bake in 400°F (200°C) oven for about 9 minutes or until fish is almost opaque. Broil for 2 to 4 minutes or until golden and fish flakes easily when tested with fork. Makes 2 servings.

TIP: Use the microwave for quick, moist fish suppers. Place fillets in a shallow glass dish and top with thinly sliced onions and lemon, or a drizzle of lemon juice, olive oil and a sprinkle of rosemary or thyme, or even a chunky tomato sauce. Cover and microwave at High for 5 minutes or until fish is just opaque.

Oven-Roasted Salmon

Author and cooking-school owner Bonnie Stern created this Moroccan-flavored salmon dish. With high-temperature roasting, one of her favorite ways to cook fish, the fish turns out moist and juicy on the inside, gloriously burnished on the outside.

Per serving: about
- 205 calories
- 11 g fat
- 21 g protein
- 5 g carbohydrate

4	salmon fillets (with skin), 1 inch (2.5 cm) thick (each 4 oz/125 g)	4
1 tbsp	liquid honey	15 mL
1 tsp	lemon juice	5 mL
1	small clove garlic, minced	1
1/2 tsp	each salt, ground cumin and paprika	2 mL
1/2 tsp	sesame oil	2 mL
Pinch	cayenne pepper	Pinch
1 tbsp	olive oil	15 mL

● Arrange fish, skin side down, in single layer in shallow glass dish. Combine honey, lemon juice, garlic, salt, cumin, paprika, sesame oil and cayenne pepper; spread over fish. Cover and marinate in refrigerator for at least 1 hour or for up to 2 hours.

● In nonstick ovenproof skillet, heat oil over high heat; cook salmon, skin side up, for 1 minute. Turn and cook for 1 minute.

● Transfer skillet to 425°F (220°C) oven; roast for 8 to 10 minutes or until fish is opaque and flakes easily when tested with fork. Makes 4 servings.

TIP: If you don't have an ovenproof skillet, wrap handle in foil. Or, transfer fish to baking sheet and roast for a few minutes longer than specified in order for heat to penetrate cool baking sheet.

Fish Fillets Dijonnaise ▲

1	slice day-old brown bread	1
2 tbsp	freshly grated Parmesan cheese	25 mL
1 tbsp	chopped fresh parsley	15 mL
8 oz	fish fillets	250 g
2 tbsp	2% plain yogurt	25 mL
2 tbsp	light mayonnaise	25 mL
1 tsp	Dijon mustard	5 mL

● In blender or food processor, crumble bread into crumbs; stir in Parmesan cheese and parsley.

● Arrange fish in single layer on greased rimmed baking sheet. Stir together yogurt, mayonnaise and mustard; spread over fish. Sprinkle evenly with crumb mixture.

● Bake in 450°F (230°C) oven for 10 to 15 minutes or just until fish is opaque and flakes easily when tested with fork. Broil for 1 to 2 minutes or until crumbs are crisp. Makes 2 servings.

T*hick fillets of pickerel, haddock, sole or turbot have more pizzazz with this lightened-up topping.*

Per serving: about
- 220 calories
- 8 g fat
- good source of calcium
- 26 g protein
- 10 g carbohydrate

Basil Salmon ◄

4	salmon fillets (with skin) (each 4 oz/125 g)	4
2 tbsp	olive oil	25 mL
2 tsp	lemon juice	10 mL
2 tsp	Dijon mustard	10 mL
2	cloves garlic, minced	2
1/4 cup	chopped fresh basil	50 mL

● Arrange fish, skin side down, in single layer in shallow glass dish. Whisk together oil, lemon juice, mustard and garlic; stir in basil. Spread over fish. Cover and marinate in refrigerator for 1 hour.

● Place fish, skin side down, on greased grill over low heat; close lid and cook for about 15 minutes or until fish is opaque and flakes easily when tested with fork. Makes 4 servings.

A slow cook on the barbecue allows such a perfect marriage of basil and salmon that you'll wonder why you never thought of pairing them before!

Per serving: about
• 215 calories • 21 g protein
• 14 g fat • 1 g carbohydrate

Boston Bluefish with Rosemary

4	Boston bluefish (pollock) fillets, 1 inch (2.5 cm) thick (each 4 oz/125 g)	4
1 tbsp	olive oil	15 mL
2 tsp	chopped fresh rosemary (or 1/2 tsp/2 mL dried)	10 mL
1/2 tsp	each pepper and salt	2 mL

● Arrange fish in single layer in shallow glass dish. Brush with oil; sprinkle with rosemary and pepper. Cover and marinate in refrigerator for 8 hours.

● Sprinkle fish with salt. Place on greased grill over medium-high heat, or on broiler pan; close lid and cook, turning once, for about 10 minutes or until fish is opaque and flakes easily when tested with fork. Makes 4 servings.

Just the simple touch of rosemary, mellowed by marinating, is enough to boost the flavor of fish to impressive heights.

Per serving: about
• 175 calories • 23 g protein
• 8 g fat • trace carbohydrate

Hoisin-Glazed Sea Bass

2 tbsp	hoisin sauce	25 mL
1 tbsp	soy sauce	15 mL
2 tsp	sesame oil	10 mL
1/4 tsp	pepper	1 mL
4	sea bass fillets, 1 inch (2.5 cm) thick (each 4 oz/125 g)	4

● In small bowl, combine hoisin sauce, soy sauce, sesame oil and pepper; spread some of the glaze over each side of fish, reserving remaining glaze for basting.

● Place fish, skin side down, on greased grill over medium-high heat, or on broiler pan; close lid and cook, basting occasionally with reserved glaze and turning once, for about 10 minutes or until fish is opaque and flakes easily when tested with fork. Makes 4 servings.

TIP: If you can't find sea bass, substitute salmon, halibut, cod, tuna or swordfish.

It's hard to believe that so few ingredients can produce such an impressive-tasting dish. Credit goes to an amazing glaze that sweetens the fish and offers an enticing touch of exotic flavor.

Per serving: about
• 130 calories • 21 g protein
• 4 g fat • 2 g carbohydrate

Broiled Fish with Parsley Chive Sauce

The microwave, darling in the kitchen a decade ago, is one handy appliance, wonderfully suited to sauce making. If your microwave has been languishing, here's a light sauce you can bubble up in it while firm, white fillets crisp in the oven.

Per serving: about
- 255 calories
- 6 g fat
- 32 g protein
- 15 g carbohydrate

1/2 cup	dry bread crumbs	125 mL
Pinch	each salt and pepper	Pinch
1 lb	white fish fillets	500 g
2 tbsp	lemon juice	25 mL
	SAUCE	
1 tbsp	butter	15 mL
1 tbsp	all-purpose flour	15 mL
1 cup	milk	250 mL
3/4 tsp	grated lemon rind	4 mL
2 tbsp	chopped fresh parsley	25 mL
1 tbsp	chopped fresh chives or green onion tops	15 mL
1/4 tsp	pepper	1 mL
Pinch	salt	Pinch

● SAUCE: In 4-cup (1 L) microwaveable measure, microwave butter at High for 30 seconds or until melted. Stir in flour; microwave at High for 1 minute, stirring once. Whisk in milk and lemon rind; microwave at High for 5 to 7 minutes or until boiling and thickened, whisking frequently. Let stand for 1 minute. Stir in parsley, chives, pepper and salt.

● Meanwhile, in shallow dish, combine bread crumbs, salt and pepper. Brush fish all over with lemon juice; dip into crumb mixture, turning to coat.

● Place fish on greased baking sheet; broil for about 5 minutes or until golden and fish is opaque and flakes easily when tested with fork. Serve with sauce. Makes 4 servings.

TIP: If using frozen fish, individually frozen pieces are more expensive but more convenient. Block-frozen fillets are cheaper but tend to be irregular in size. Fresh fillets are most flavorful and are also more even in size for more even cooking.

Steamed Fish for Two

This Asian-inspired method of steaming fish on top of vegetables keeps flavors fresh, colors bright and fat healthfully low. Add a side of whole-grain brown or parboiled rice.

Per serving: about
- 460 calories
- 30 g fat
- very high source of fiber
- 25 g protein
- 26 g carbohydrate
- good source of iron

1	small bulb fennel	1
Half	small Spanish onion	Half
8 oz	salmon, red snapper or Boston bluefish fillet	250 g
Pinch	each salt and pepper	Pinch
1 tsp	olive oil	5 mL
2	carrots, thinly sliced	2
1 cup	snow peas	250 mL
	VINAIGRETTE	
2 tbsp	lemon juice	25 mL
1 tbsp	white wine vinegar	15 mL
1 tsp	Dijon mustard	5 mL
1/2 tsp	granulated sugar	2 mL
1/2 tsp	each salt and pepper	2 mL
3 tbsp	olive oil	50 mL

● Trim fronds from fennel; set aside. Cut fennel bulb in half lengthwise; thinly slice bulb and stalks crosswise. Cut onion in half crosswise; slice each half thinly. Cut fish in half; sprinkle with salt and pepper.

● In large nonstick skillet, heat oil over medium heat; cook carrots, fennel and onion, stirring, for 1 minute. Reduce heat to medium-low; cook, stirring occasionally, for about 15 minutes or until softened.

● VINAIGRETTE: Chop reserved fennel fronds. In bowl, whisk together lemon juice, vinegar, mustard, sugar, salt, pepper and fronds; gradually whisk in oil.

● Stir 2 tbsp (25 mL) of the vinaigrette into skillet along with snow peas; top with fish. Cover and cook for about 12 minutes or just until fish is opaque and flakes easily when tested with fork. Serve with remaining vinaigrette drizzled over top. Makes 2 servings.

Tuna Burgers ▲

2	eggs	2
1/3 cup	dry bread crumbs	75 mL
1 tbsp	chopped fresh dill (or 1 tsp/5 mL dried dillweed)	15 mL
1 tbsp	prepared horseradish	15 mL
2 tsp	Dijon mustard	10 mL
1/4 tsp	pepper	1 mL
Pinch	salt	Pinch
2	cans (each 6.5 oz/184 g) water-packed tuna	2
2	green onions, minced	2
1	stalk celery, chopped	1
1 tbsp	vegetable oil	15 mL
	Alfalfa sprouts	
4	whole wheat hamburger buns	4

● In bowl, lightly beat eggs; mix in bread crumbs, dill, horseradish, mustard, pepper and salt. Drain tuna; mix into bowl along with green onions and celery. Shape into four 1/2-inch (1 cm) thick patties.

● In nonstick skillet, heat oil over medium heat; cook patties, turning once, for about 10 minutes or until golden brown and set. Sandwich along with alfalfa sprouts in buns. Makes 4 servings.

There are a few staples that should be in every cupboard, and canned tuna is certainly one of them. It makes splendid sandwiches, melts, salads and, here, golden brown "burgers" to enjoy on a bun with sprouts and whatever else catches your fancy.

Per serving: about
- 360 calories
- 9 g fat
- high source of fiber
- 32 g protein
- 40 g carbohydrate
- good source of iron

Cod Braised in Tomato Sauce

Fish bakes to perfection under an Italian-inspired tomato sauce. Any thick, firm, white-fleshed fish, such as halibut or monkfish, is also delicious cooked this way.

Per serving: about
- 165 calories
- 22 g protein
- 5 g fat
- 9 g carbohydrate

1 tbsp	olive oil	15 mL
1	onion, chopped	1
1	clove garlic, finely chopped	1
Pinch	hot pepper flakes	Pinch
1	can (19 oz/540 mL) tomatoes	1
1/2 tsp	each salt and pepper	2 mL
1 lb	cod fillets, cut in 4 pieces	500 g
2 tbsp	chopped fresh parsley	25 mL

● In large deep skillet, heat oil over medium heat; cook onion, garlic and hot pepper flakes, stirring occasionally, for about 5 minutes or until softened.

● Add tomatoes, breaking up with fork; bring to boil. Cook over medium-high heat, uncovered and stirring often, for about 20 minutes or until thickened. Season with salt and pepper.

● Arrange fish in single layer in sauce, spooning sauce over top. Cover and cook over medium-high heat for about 8 minutes or until fish is opaque and flakes easily when tested with fork. Serve sprinkled with parsley. Makes 4 servings.

Niçoise Heroes ▼

When work or heat has zapped your energy, sandwiches come to the supper rescue. A tuna, tomato, basil and black olive combination from Nice — hence Niçoise — is menu inspiration.

Per serving: about
- 370 calories
- 28 g protein
- 9 g fat
- 43 g carbohydrate
- good source of iron

1/4 cup	light mayonnaise	50 mL	2	cans (each 6 oz/170 g) water-packed solid tuna	2
1/4 cup	light sour cream	50 mL	2	green onions, chopped	2
1 tsp	Dijon mustard	5 mL	1 cup	alfalfa sprouts	250 mL
Pinch	pepper	Pinch			
4	hero or Italian buns	4			
6	black olives, chopped	6			
4	lettuce leaves	4			
1	tomato, sliced	1			

● In bowl, stir together mayonnaise, sour cream, mustard and pepper. Cut buns in half horizontally; spread each half with about 1 tsp (5 mL) of the mayonnaise mixture. Sprinkle olives over bottom halves; top each with lettuce leaf and tomato slices.

● Drain tuna well; stir into remaining mayonnaise mixture and break into chunks. Add onions; stir until moistened. Spoon over tomatoes; add sprouts and bun tops. Makes 4 servings.

FAVORITE FISH TOPPINGS

Fish and fish cakes need a touch of tangy sauce to perk them up. Here's a tasty trio worth trying.

Mustard-Dill Sauce
● In small saucepan, bring 2/3 cup (150 mL) light cream to boil. Dissolve 1 tbsp (15 mL) cornstarch in 1 tbsp (15 mL) water; whisk into cream and cook, whisking, until thickened and smooth. Stir in 1/3 cup (75 mL) white wine, 1 tbsp (15 mL) chopped fresh dill and 2 tsp (10 mL) Dijon mustard. Season with

salt and pepper to taste. Makes 1 cup (250 mL).

Light Tartar Sauce
● Combine 2/3 cup (150 mL) plain low-fat yogurt, 1/4 cup (50 mL) relish, 2 tbsp (25 mL) light mayonnaise and 1 tsp (5 mL) each red wine vinegar and Dijon mustard. Makes about 1 cup (250 mL).

Salsa Mexicana
● In 2-cup (500 mL) microwaveable measure, combine 1 finely chopped small onion, 1 clove garlic, minced, and 1 tbsp (15 mL) vegetable oil; microwave at High for 2 minutes or until onion is softened. Stir in 1 cup (250 mL) chopped drained canned tomatoes and

1/4 tsp (1 mL) hot pepper flakes; microwave at High for 3 to 4 minutes or until heated through. Stir in 1 tbsp (15 mL) finely chopped coriander or parsley. Season with salt to taste. Serve hot or cold. Makes 1 cup (250 mL).

Crispy Fish Cakes

1	large baking potato, peeled and quartered	1
1 lb	fish fillets	500 g
1	egg	1
1/4 cup	minced green onion	50 mL
2 tbsp	minced fresh parsley	25 mL
1 tbsp	chopped fresh dill	15 mL
1 tbsp	light mayonnaise	15 mL
1/2 tsp	salt	2 mL
1/4 tsp	pepper	1 mL
Dash	hot pepper sauce	Dash
1/2 cup	dry bread crumbs	125 mL
2 tbsp	vegetable oil	25 mL

● In saucepan of boiling salted water, cook potato for 17 to 20 minutes or until tender. Remove with slotted spoon; drain and mash. Set aside.

● In same water, poach fillets over medium-low heat for 5 minutes or until fish flakes easily when tested with fork; drain and process in food processor until smooth.

● In bowl, beat egg; stir in mashed potato, fish, onion, parsley, dill, mayonnaise, salt, pepper and hot pepper sauce. Form into 8 patties, 1/2 inch (1 cm) thick. In shallow dish, press patties into bread crumbs to coat all over.

● In large nonstick skillet, heat oil over medium-high heat; cook patties for 3 minutes. Using two spatulas, turn carefully; cook for 2 or 3 minutes longer or until golden brown. Makes 4 servings.

TIP: Leftover mashed potatoes can be used instead of baking and mashing a fresh potato. You need about 1 cup (250 mL).

Their crisp golden outsides around a moist, fragrant blend of fish, herbs and potatoes make fish cakes perennial family favorites. For more kid-appeal, shape the cakes to look like fish. Serve with crisp carrot sticks, broccoli and cauliflower florets and a light tartar sauce.

Per serving: about
● 275 calories ● 26 g protein
● 11 g fat ● 18 g carbohydrate
● good source of iron

Vegetarian Family Favorites

With appetizing grain-, rice- and legume-based main dishes, it's easy to prepare meatless meals the whole family will enjoy. That's great news for the cook, too — no more extra planning, shopping and preparation especially for the meat abstainer in the family or for a dinner guest who's vegetarian.

Asparagus Risotto ▶

Although traditional risotto requires constant stirring, this labor-saving cheater's version is just the thing for busy cooks. The Arborio rice is covered and partially cooked, with only an occasional stir, then finished off with stock and cheese.

Per serving: about
- 430 calories
- 10 g fat
- good source of iron
- 16 g protein
- 69 g carbohydrate

1 tbsp	olive oil	15 mL
2 cups	sliced mushrooms (1/3 lb/170 g)	500 mL
2	cloves garlic, minced	2
1	onion, chopped	1
1/2 tsp	pepper	2 mL
1/4 tsp	salt	1 mL
1-1/2 cups	Arborio or other Italian short-grain rice	375 mL
4 cups	vegetable or chicken stock	1 L
1 tbsp	white wine vinegar	15 mL
1 lb	asparagus	500 g
1/2 tsp	grated lemon rind	2 mL
1/2 cup	freshly grated Asiago or Parmesan cheese	125 mL

● In large heavy saucepan, heat oil over medium-high heat; cook mushrooms, garlic, onion, pepper and salt, stirring, for about 4 minutes or until mushrooms are browned and moisture is evaporated.

● Stir in rice, 3-1/2 cups (875 mL) of the stock and vinegar; bring to boil. Cover and reduce heat to low; simmer for 10 minutes.

● Meanwhile, trim asparagus; cut diagonally into 1-inch (2.5 cm) lengths. Add to pan along with lemon rind. Cook, covered, for 10 minutes or until liquid is almost absorbed, asparagus is tender-crisp and rice is still slightly firm to the bite.

● Stir in remaining stock and Asiago cheese until mixture is creamy. Serve immediately. Makes 4 servings.

MEATLESS MAIN COURSES

It's easier to create main-course vegetarian dishes than you think.

● Instead of flavoring soups, salads and pastas with a bit of chopped smoked ham, chicken or turkey or crumbled bacon, use more herbs or extra spices, instead.
● Replace chicken stock with vegetable stock.

● Toss cooked beans, chick-peas, lentils or cubed firm tofu into vegetables-only salads, soups, stir-fries, casseroles and pasta sauces.

Pepper Corn Paella

*A*ll you need is a skillet, fresh vegetables and a short- or medium-grain rice such as Italian Arborio to make this satisfying supper. Add a crisp green salad and crusty whole wheat rolls.

Per serving: about
- 305 calories
- 4 g fat
- 7 g protein
- 61 g carbohydrate

1 tbsp	vegetable oil	15 mL
1	onion, chopped	1
2	cloves garlic, minced	2
1 cup	short-grain rice	250 mL
1/4 tsp	turmeric	1 mL
2 cups	warm vegetable stock	500 mL
1/4 tsp	each salt and pepper	1 mL
1	each sweet green and red pepper	1
2	plum tomatoes	2
1-1/2 cups	corn kernels	375 mL
	Chopped fresh parsley	

● In large nonstick skillet or paella pan, heat oil over medium heat; cook onion, garlic, rice and turmeric, stirring occasionally, for 4 minutes or until onion is softened.

● Stir in stock, salt and pepper; bring to boil. Reduce heat, cover and simmer for 10 minutes.

● Meanwhile, seed, core and cut green and red peppers in half lengthwise. Cut in half crosswise; cut lengthwise into strips. Core and chop tomatoes.

● Add peppers and tomatoes to pan; cook, covered, for 15 minutes or until rice is almost tender. Stir in corn; cook, covered, for about 5 minutes or until liquid is evaporated. Serve garnished with parsley. Makes 4 servings.

Bean Fajitas

*F*or lovers of Southwestern flavors, here's a hot-and-spicy, all-vegetable version of fajitas to wrap up in warm tortillas or pita breads.

Per serving: about
- 805 calories
- 19 g fat
- very high source of fiber
- 35 g protein
- 127 g carbohydrate
- excellent source of calcium and iron

2 tsp	vegetable oil	10 mL
1	onion, chopped	1
Half	sweet red or green pepper, chopped	Half
1	small zucchini, chopped	1
2	cloves garlic, slivered	2
1-1/2 tsp	chili powder	7 mL
1/2 tsp	ground cumin	2 mL
1	can (19 oz/540 mL) black beans, drained and rinsed	1
1/4 cup	chunky salsa	50 mL
1/4 cup	chopped fresh coriander (optional)	50 mL
4	large (9-inch/23 cm) flour tortillas	4
1/3 cup	each shredded lettuce, chopped tomato, low-fat plain yogurt and shredded Monterey Jack cheese	75 mL

● In large nonstick skillet, heat oil over medium heat; cook onion, red pepper, zucchini, garlic, chili powder and cumin, stirring occasionally, for about 7 minutes or until softened.

● Add black beans and salsa; cook for about 5 minutes or just until moisture is evaporated. Stir in coriander (if using).

● Meanwhile, wrap tortillas in foil; heat in 300°F (150°C) oven for about 10 minutes or just until warm.

● Divide bean mixture among tortillas; sprinkle with lettuce and tomato. Dollop each with yogurt; sprinkle with Monterey Jack cheese and roll up. Makes 2 servings.

TIP: You can use other beans — red kidney, romano or pinto — or a combination of varieties. If you are soaking and cooking dry beans, start with 1 cup (250 mL) beans to get 2 cups (500 mL) cooked, the amount most 19-ounce (540 mL) cans contain.

Tempeh Chili ▲

1 tbsp	vegetable oil	15 mL
12 oz	tempeh, thawed and crumbled	375 g
1	onion, chopped	1
Half	sweet green pepper, chopped	Half
2	cloves garlic, minced	2
1	can (28 oz/796 mL) tomatoes	1
1	can (19 oz/540 mL) kidney beans, drained and rinsed	1
1	can (5-1/2 oz/156 mL) tomato paste	1
1/4 cup	cider vinegar	50 mL
1/4 cup	molasses	50 mL
1 tbsp	soy sauce	15 mL
1 tbsp	Dijon mustard	15 mL
2 tsp	chili powder	10 mL
1 tsp	each dried basil and oregano	5 mL
1/2 tsp	salt	2 mL
1/4 tsp	pepper	1 mL

● In large saucepan, heat oil over medium heat; cook tempeh with 1/2 cup (125 mL) water, stirring, for about 5 minutes or until browned.

● Add onion, green pepper and garlic; cover and cook, stirring occasionally, for 5 minutes or until onion is softened.

● Chop tomatoes and add with juices. Add kidney beans, tomato paste, vinegar, molasses, soy sauce, mustard, chili powder, basil, oregano, salt and pepper to pan; bring to boil. Reduce heat and simmer for 15 minutes. Makes 6 servings.

Tempeh, a fermented soybean patty with a meaty texture and mild flavor, is high in protein. Look for it in the freezer section of health-food stores. It resembles puffed rice stuck together, but crumbles very easily into vegetable stews, stir-fries — or this chili.

Per serving: about
- 312 calories
- 19 g protein
- 8 g fat
- 47 g carbohydrate
- very high source of fiber
- excellent source of iron

Rice and Beans

Rice cooked with dried beans and bright healthful vegetables picks up Caribbean vibes of thyme, allspice and a nose-tweaking dash of hot pepper sauce.

Per serving: about
- 418 calories
- 5 g fat
- very high source of fiber
- 15 g protein
- 80 g carbohydrate
- good source of iron

2 tsp	vegetable oil	10 mL
3	cloves garlic, minced	3
2	carrots, diced	2
1	onion, chopped	1
1 tsp	dried thyme	5 mL
Pinch	ground allspice	Pinch
1-1/4 cups	long-grain rice	300 mL
2-1/4 cups	vegetable stock	550 mL
1/4 tsp	hot pepper sauce	1 mL
1	can (19 oz/540 mL) black beans, drained and rinsed	1
1	sweet green pepper, diced	1
1/3 cup	plain yogurt	75 mL
	Chopped fresh parsley	

● In nonstick skillet, heat oil over medium heat; cook garlic, carrots, onion, thyme and allspice, stirring occasionally, for about 5 minutes or until onion is softened.

● Stir in rice; cook for 1 minute, stirring. Stir in stock and hot pepper sauce; bring to boil. Reduce heat, cover and simmer for 20 minutes or until liquid is almost absorbed.

● Stir in black beans and green pepper; cook, covered, for 7 minutes or until beans are hot and green pepper is tender-crisp. Serve topped with yogurt and sprinkled with parsley. Makes 4 servings.

Grilled Tofu

Tofu is the great flavor absorber, and it needs a zesty marinade like this one. Serve with seasonal vegetables and a salad.

Per serving: about
- 190 calories
- 10 g fat
- excellent source of calcium and iron
- 18 g protein
- 11 g carbohydrate

1	pkg (1 lb/450 g) firm tofu	1
2 tbsp	soy sauce	25 mL
1 tbsp	packed brown sugar	15 mL
1 tbsp	ketchup	15 mL
1 tbsp	prepared horseradish	15 mL
1 tbsp	cider vinegar	15 mL
1	clove garlic, minced	1

● Cut tofu into 1/2-inch (1 cm) thick slices; place in single layer in shallow glass dish. Whisk together soy sauce, brown sugar, ketchup, horseradish, vinegar and garlic; pour over tofu, turning to coat. Cover and marinate at room temperature for 1 hour or in refrigerator for up to 24 hours, turning occasionally.

● Reserving marinade, place tofu on greased grill over medium-high heat; close lid and cook, turning once and basting with marinade, for about 6 minutes or until browned. Makes 4 servings.

VEGETARIAN STAPLES

To make vegetarian meals quicker and easier to cook, have on hand:
● Rice, pasta, chick-peas and lentils.
● Barley, kasha, cracked wheat, bulgur and couscous.
● Nuts and seeds.

● Dried fruits such as apricots, figs, dates, apples and prunes.
● Dried mushrooms.
● Herbs and spices.
● Vinegars and oils.
● Vegetable stock. Refrigerate some of your own

short-term from cooking mild vegetables such as carrots and potatoes.
● Canned tomatoes and paste; canned corn, beets and artichokes; roasted peppers.
● In the refrigerator or freezer — tahini, peanut and other

nut butters, cheeses, eggs, milk, yogurt, tortillas, whole-wheat pita breads, ready-to-top-and-bake pizza bases, hummus, tofu, tempeh, plenty of sprouts and fresh and frozen fruits and vegetables.

Cajun Tofu Kabobs

1	pkg (1 lb/450 g) firm tofu	1
1/4 cup	tomato juice	50 mL
1 tbsp	vegetable oil	15 mL
1 tsp	paprika	5 mL
1/2 tsp	each salt, pepper and chili powder	2 mL
1/2 tsp	each dried oregano, thyme and dry mustard	2 mL
1/4 tsp	Worcestershire sauce	1 mL
Dash	hot pepper sauce	Dash

● Cut tofu into 1-1/2- x 1-inch (4 x 2.5 cm) cubes; place in shallow dish and set aside.

● In microwaveable measure or saucepan, combine tomato juice, oil, paprika, salt, pepper, chili powder, oregano, thyme, mustard, Worcestershire sauce and hot pepper sauce; microwave at High for 1 minute or heat on stove top until boiling. Brush over tofu, turning to coat evenly.

● Cover and marinate at room temperature for 1 hour or in refrigerator for up to 8 hours.

● Thread cubes evenly onto four 8-inch (20 cm) soaked wooden skewers. Place on greased grill over medium-high heat; close lid and cook, turning occasionally, for about 20 minutes or until browned and heated through. Makes 4 servings.

These Bayou-flavored kabobs are delicious served over rice or couscous and lavished with Fresh Plum Tomato Sauce (below).

Per serving: about
- 205 calories
- 14 g fat
- good source of calcium
- 18 g protein
- 6 g carbohydrate
- excellent source of iron

TIPS

● When grilling tofu, be sure to use the type marked "firm" or "firmer" so it will hold together well on the barbecue.

● Soak wooden skewers for 30 minutes before threading with tofu, vegetables, meat, fish or poultry. This prevents the wood from catching fire when the kabobs are grilled.

Fresh Plum Tomato Sauce

4 cups	chopped plum tomatoes, about 8 (1-3/4 lb/875 g)	1 L
4	cloves garlic, minced	4
1/4 cup	chopped fresh basil (or 4 tsp/20 mL dried)	50 mL
2 tbsp	vegetable oil	25 mL
1 tbsp	balsamic or red wine vinegar	15 mL
1/4 tsp	each salt and pepper	1 mL

● In bowl, gently stir together tomatoes, garlic, basil, oil, vinegar, salt and pepper. Spoon onto center of large piece of heavy-duty foil; fold up foil and seal tightly to form packet. Overwrap with another piece of foil.

● Place on grill over medium-high heat; close lid and cook, turning once, for about 25 minutes or until tomatoes are very soft. Makes 4 servings.

This chunky basil-blessed tomato sauce cooks on the barbecue alongside the Cajun Tofu Kabobs (above) but could just as easily be simmered in a saucepan.

Per serving: about
- 110 calories
- 7 g fat
- 2 g protein
- 11 g carbohydrate

TIP: If you choose a saucepan and fresh plum tomatoes aren't worth buying, use 1 can (28 oz/796 mL) tomatoes with their juices. Chop the tomatoes coarsely right in the can. All commercially canned tomatoes are now plum-type.

Broccoli and Cheese Strata

1 cup	coarsely chopped broccoli	250 mL
2	green onions, sliced	2
2	slices bread, cubed	2
1/2 cup	shredded Cheddar cheese	125 mL
2	eggs	2
1/2 cup	1% milk	125 mL
1 tbsp	chopped fresh dill	15 mL
1/2 tsp	Dijon mustard	2 mL
Pinch	each pepper and nutmeg	Pinch

● In microwaveable bowl, microwave broccoli, green onions and 1 tbsp (15 mL) water at High for 1 minute. Drain and set aside.

● Divide bread cubes between two lightly greased 4-inch (10 cm) ramekins or 1-cup (250 mL) ovenproof dishes. Divide broccoli mixture between ramekins; sprinkle evenly with Cheddar.

● Blend together eggs, milk, dill, mustard, pepper and nutmeg; pour over cheese. Cover and refrigerate for at least 1 hour or for up to 12 hours.

● Bake, uncovered, in 350°F (180°C) oven for about 20 minutes or until set in center. Let stand for 5 minutes. Makes 2 servings.

*W*hether you serve it for a quick supper or for lunch, this cheesy, broccoli-dotted bread pudding — that's what a "strata" is — looks and tastes impressive. Add a plate lined with Boston or romaine lettuce and piled with tomato and cucumber slices, and you have a delicious dinner just for two.

Per serving: about
- 310 calories
- 19 g protein
- 16 g fat
- 21 g carbohydrate
- excellent source of calcium

Southwestern Sandwiches ◄

1 tsp	vegetable oil	5 mL
1/4 cup	each chopped sweet red pepper and zucchini	50 mL
1/4 cup	corn kernels	50 mL
1/4 tsp	each salt and pepper	1 mL
8	eggs, beaten	8
Pinch	chili powder (optional)	Pinch
4	large (9-inch/23 cm) flour tortillas or pita breads	4
4	leaves leaf lettuce	4
1/4 cup	medium salsa	50 mL
	GUACAMOLE	
Half	avocado	Half
2 tbsp	lemon juice	25 mL
1	small clove garlic, minced	1
Dash	hot pepper sauce	Dash
	Salt and pepper	

● In nonstick skillet, heat oil over medium heat; cook red pepper, zucchini, corn, salt and pepper, stirring occasionally, for about 3 minutes or until softened.

● Pour in eggs; cook, stirring, for 3 minutes. Cover and cook, without stirring, for about 4 minutes or until eggs are just set. Remove from heat. Sprinkle with chili powder (if using). Cut into 4 strips.

● GUACAMOLE: Meanwhile, peel avocado and place in bowl. Add lemon juice, garlic, hot pepper sauce, and salt and pepper to taste; mash until combined.

● Spread guacamole evenly over tortillas right to edge; top each with lettuce leaf. Place egg strip down center; roll up tortilla. Serve with salsa. Makes 4 servings.

*E*ggs come to the rescue for a fast, healthful supper — spruced up with guacamole and rolled in a trendy tortilla. Add some crunch to the menu with sprouts, radishes and slices of cucumber.

Per serving: about
- 400 calories
- 19 g protein
- 18 g fat
- 41 g carbohydrate
- excellent source of iron

Vegetable Frittata ▲

Good-for-you-vegetables such as broccoli and sweet potatoes pack handily into a puffy frittata sprinkled with cheese. Serve this comforting supper with whole-grain bread and a green salad.

Per serving: about
- 205 calories
- 14 g protein
- 10 g fat
- 15 g carbohydrate

1	sweet potato (8 oz/250 g)	1
2 cups	chopped broccoli	500 mL
4	eggs	4
4	egg whites	4
1/2 tsp	salt	2 mL
1/4 tsp	pepper	1 mL
2 tsp	vegetable oil	10 mL
1/4 cup	chopped green onions	50 mL
2	cloves garlic, minced	2
1 tsp	dried tarragon	5 mL
1/4 cup	shredded fontina cheese	50 mL

● Peel sweet potato; cut into 1/2-inch (1 cm) cubes. Place in steamer basket over boiling water; cover and cook for 5 minutes. Add broccoli; cook, covered, for 4 minutes or until potato is tender and broccoli is tender-crisp; set aside.

● Meanwhile, in bowl, whisk together eggs, egg whites, salt and pepper; set aside.

● In 9-inch (23 cm) ovenproof skillet, heat oil over medium heat; cook onions, garlic and tarragon, stirring, for about 2 minutes or until softened.

● Spread sweet potato mixture in skillet; pour egg mixture over top. Reduce heat to medium-low; cover and cook for about 12 minutes or until bottom is golden and edge is set but center still jiggles slightly. Sprinkle with fontina cheese; broil for 2 to 3 minutes or until light golden and cheese is bubbly. Makes 4 servings.

Pizza Pronto!

12 oz	frozen pizza dough	375 g
1 cup	shredded part-skim mozzarella cheese	250 mL
1	can (14 oz/398 mL) artichokes, drained and quartered	1
1 cup	thinly sliced Spanish onion	250 mL
2	tomatoes, sliced	2
1	roasted sweet red or green pepper, sliced	1
2 tsp	dried basil	10 mL
1 oz	chèvre (cream goat cheese), crumbled	30 g
Pinch	hot pepper flakes	Pinch

● On lightly floured surface, roll out pizza dough to fit 17- x 11-inch (45 x 29 cm) baking sheet.

● Sprinkle with mozzarella cheese, artichokes and onion. Top with tomatoes and red pepper. Sprinkle with basil, chèvre and hot pepper flakes.

● Bake on bottom rack in 500°F (260°C) oven for 15 minutes or until cheese is bubbly and crust is golden. Makes 6 servings.

TIP: To roast sweet pepper, grill or broil, turning often, for 20 to 25 minutes or until charred. Let cool slightly; peel, seed and slice.

This favorite brunch dish from author Anne Lindsay also makes an excellent spur-of-the-moment supper. Just top a pizza base with mozzarella, fresh tomatoes, Spanish onion and roasted pepper, then pop into the oven until bubbly and golden. Artichoke hearts add a tantalizing twist.

Per serving: about
- 265 calories
- 7 g fat
- high source of fiber
- 13 g protein
- 38 g carbohydrate
- good source of calcium and iron

Pizza Primavera

1	round (12-inch/30 cm) prebaked pizza crust or focaccia bread	1
2 cups	shredded fontina or Danbo cheese	500 mL
1 lb	fresh asparagus	500 g
1 tbsp	olive oil	15 mL
2	cloves garlic, minced	2
1	red onion, thinly sliced	1
1	sweet red pepper, thinly sliced	1
1/3 cup	chopped fresh basil or parsley	75 mL
1 tbsp	chopped pickled hot pepper (optional)	15 mL
1/4 tsp	pepper	1 mL

● Place pizza crust on baking sheet; sprinkle with half of the fontina cheese. Set aside. Trim and cut asparagus into 2-inch (5 cm) pieces. Set aside.

● In large skillet, heat oil over medium heat; cook garlic and onion, stirring occasionally, for about 6 minutes or until softened. Add red pepper, 2 tbsp (25 mL) of the basil, and pickled hot pepper (if using); cook for 3 minutes.

● Add asparagus; cook for 3 minutes or just until bright green. Season with pepper. Spoon evenly over pizza crust; sprinkle with remaining fontina cheese.

● Bake in 400°F (200°C) oven for 15 to 20 minutes or just until cheese is bubbly. Sprinkle with remaining basil. Makes 8 wedges.

Asparagus among the toppings gives this easy pizza an undeniable hit of springtime flavor. When these stalks aren't in season, green beans add color and a pleasing crunch.

Per wedge: about
- 255 calories
- 12 g fat
- good source of calcium
- 12 g protein
- 25 g carbohydrate

Pasta to the Rescue

Despite our best intentions, it isn't always possible to have supper planned, with ingredients ready and waiting when we walk in the door at the end of a busy day. That's why smart cooks always keep a stock of pasta and sauces on hand — along with these easy recipes for turning a pantry staple into a supper sensation.

Pasta with Peppers ▶

This tasty spaghetti-sauce update is easy enough for beginner cooks — and a great way to get older children involved in mealtime preparation.

Per serving: about
- 500 calories
- 19 g protein
- 10 g fat
- 84 g carbohydrate
- very high source of fiber
- good source of calcium
- excellent source of iron

1 tbsp	olive oil	15 mL
1	onion, chopped	1
2	cloves garlic, minced	2
Pinch	hot pepper flakes	Pinch
1	can (28 oz/796 mL) tomatoes	1
2	each sweet red and green peppers, cut in strips	2
1 tsp	salt	5 mL
1/2 tsp	pepper	2 mL
12 oz	spaghetti	375 g
1/2 cup	freshly grated Parmesan cheese	125 mL
1/4 cup	pitted black olives	50 mL
2 tbsp	chopped fresh parsley	25 mL

● In large deep skillet, heat oil over medium heat; cook onion, garlic and hot pepper flakes, stirring occasionally, for 5 minutes or until softened.

● Add tomatoes, breaking up with spoon. Add red and green peppers; bring to boil. Reduce heat to medium; cook, uncovered, for 10 to 15 minutes or until thickened slightly. Season with salt and pepper.

● Meanwhile, in large pot of boiling salted water, cook spaghetti for 8 to 10 minutes or until tender but firm. Drain well and return to pot. Add sauce, Parmesan cheese, olives and parsley; toss to coat. Makes 4 servings.

Bacon and Tomato Toss

The flavor cue here is the ever-popular BLT sandwich — bacon and tomato in the pasta, with lettuce in a salad alongside.

Per serving: about
- 540 calories
- 20 g protein
- 9 g fat
- 94 g carbohydrate
- very high source of fiber
- good source of iron

8	slices bacon, chopped	8
1	onion, chopped	1
3	cloves garlic, minced	3
1 tsp	dried thyme	5 mL
1	can (19 oz/540 mL) tomatoes	1
1/4 tsp	each salt and pepper	1 mL
1/4 cup	chopped fresh parsley	50 mL
6 cups	medium pasta shells (1 lb/500 g)	1.5 L

● In skillet, cook bacon, onion, garlic and thyme, stirring often, for 5 to 7 minutes or until bacon is browned. Pour off fat.

● Add tomatoes and juices, breaking up tomatoes with spoon. Add salt and pepper; bring to boil. Reduce heat to medium; cook, uncovered, for 10 to 12 minutes or until thickened. Stir in parsley.

● Meanwhile, in large pot of boiling salted water, cook pasta for 8 to 10 minutes or until tender but firm; drain well and return to pot. Add sauce; toss to coat. Makes 4 servings.

Pasta with Spinach and Potatoes ▲

Never!" you say to anchovies. "Not on your life!" you reply to garlic. Just wait till you taste how these usually assertive raw flavors mellow and meld as they cook. We guarantee you'll change from complainer to converted after the first bite!

Per serving: about
- 630 calories
- 18 g fat
- very high source of fiber
- excellent source of iron
- 21 g protein
- 97 g carbohydrate
- good source of calcium

1	large baking potato, peeled and diced	1
5-1/2 cups	orecchiette or fusilli (1 lb/500 g)	1.375 L
1	pkg fresh spinach, coarsely chopped (10 oz/300 g)	1
1/4 cup	olive oil	50 mL
4	cloves garlic, minced	4
1 tbsp	anchovy paste (or 5 anchovies, minced)	15 mL
1/4 tsp	pepper	1 mL
Pinch	hot pepper flakes	Pinch
1/4 cup	freshly grated Parmesan cheese	50 mL

● In large pot of boiling salted water, cook potato and pasta for 6 minutes. Stir in spinach; cook for 2 to 4 minutes or until pasta is tender but firm. Reserving 1/3 cup (75 mL) cooking water, drain pasta mixture and return to pot.

● Meanwhile, in skillet, heat oil over low heat; cook garlic, stirring often, for about 5 minutes or until softened. Stir in anchovy paste, pepper and hot pepper flakes until well combined.

● Add garlic mixture and reserved cooking water to pasta mixture; toss to coat. Serve sprinkled with Parmesan cheese. Makes 4 servings.

Creamy Pasta with Peas

1 tbsp	butter	15 mL
2	small cloves garlic, minced	2
3	green onions, chopped	3
1 tbsp	all-purpose flour	15 mL
1 cup	milk	250 mL
2/3 cup	chicken or vegetable stock	150 mL
4 oz	herbed cream cheese	125 g
1/4 tsp	each salt and pepper	1 mL
12 oz	fettuccine	375 g
1-1/2 cups	frozen peas	375 mL
2 tbsp	chopped fresh chives or green onion	25 mL

● In small saucepan or nonstick skillet, melt butter over medium heat; cook garlic and onions, stirring occasionally, for 3 minutes or until softened.

● Sprinkle with flour; cook, stirring, for 1 minute. Whisk in milk and stock; cook, stirring, for 3 to 5 minutes or until thickened slightly. Stir in cheese, stirring until melted. Season with salt and pepper.

● Meanwhile, in large pot of boiling salted water, cook fettuccine for 8 minutes. Add peas; cook for 1 to 2 minutes or until pasta is tender but firm. Drain well and return to pot. Add sauce; toss to coat well. Serve sprinkled with chives. Makes 4 servings.

TIP: When it's adults only, replace half the herbed cream cheese with a creamy Canadian goat cheese, with or without herbs.

It's worth stocking herbed cream cheese in the fridge and peas in the freezer for this quick dish.

Per serving: about
- 540 calories
- 17 g fat
- very high source of fiber
- 19 g protein
- 77 g carbohydrate
- good source of iron

Easy Creamy Turkey Fettuccine

2 tsp	olive oil	10 mL
2 cups	sliced mushrooms (6 oz/175 g)	500 mL
1 cup	chopped red onion	250 mL
1 cup	sliced celery	250 mL
3	cloves garlic, minced	3
1-1/2 cups	cooked turkey strips	375 mL
1 cup	2% evaporated milk	250 mL
1/4 cup	chopped fresh parsley	50 mL
1/4 cup	packed chopped fresh basil (or 2 tsp/10 mL dried)	50 mL
1/4 cup	freshly grated Parmesan cheese	50 mL
1/2 tsp	salt	2 mL
1/4 tsp	pepper	1 mL
6 oz	fettuccine or spaghetti	175 g

● In large saucepan, heat oil over medium heat; cook mushrooms, onion, celery and garlic, stirring occasionally, for 8 to 10 minutes or until vegetables are tender. Stir in turkey, milk, parsley, basil, Parmesan cheese, salt and pepper.

● Meanwhile, in large pot of boiling salted water, cook pasta for 8 to 10 minutes or until tender but firm. Drain well and return to pot. Add sauce; simmer, stirring gently, for 3 minutes. Makes 2 servings.

Perfect for the day after Thanksgiving or Christmas, this inventive pasta dish makes a feast of turkey leftovers. Low-fat creaminess comes from 2% evaporated milk.

Per serving: about
- 770 calories
- 18 g fat
- very high source of fiber
- 60 g protein
- 92 g carbohydrate
- excellent source of calcium and iron

Mushroom Linguine

For people with a lactose intolerance, soy milk allows them to enjoy "creamy" sauces without the cream. Lean ham, herbs such as thyme and a bounty of mushrooms more than compensate for the dairy taste that can't be there.

Per serving: about
- 620 calories
- 28 g protein
- 13 g fat
- 96 g carbohydrate
- very high source of fiber
- excellent source of iron

2 tbsp	olive oil	25 mL
1	onion, chopped	1
1	clove garlic, minced	1
6 cups	sliced mushrooms	1.5 L
1 tsp	dried thyme	5 mL
1/4 tsp	nutmeg	1 mL
2 tbsp	all-purpose flour	25 mL
2 cups	soy milk or 2% milk	500 mL
1 lb	linguine or spaghetti	500 g
1 cup	cubed Black Forest ham (about 7 oz/200 g)	250 mL
1/2 cup	chopped fresh parsley	125 mL
3/4 tsp	salt	4 mL
1/2 tsp	pepper	2 mL

● In large skillet, heat oil over medium heat; cook onion and garlic, stirring occasionally, for 5 minutes or until softened. Add mushrooms, thyme and nutmeg; cook, stirring occasionally, for 5 minutes or until most of the moisture is evaporated.

● Sprinkle with flour; cook, stirring, for 1 minute. Whisk in milk; cook, stirring often, for 12 minutes or until thickened.

● Meanwhile, in large pot of boiling salted water, cook linguine for 8 to 10 minutes or until tender but firm. Drain well and return to pot. Add sauce, ham, 1/3 cup (75 mL) of the parsley, salt and pepper; toss to coat. Serve sprinkled with remaining parsley. Makes 4 servings.

Creamy Penne with Tomatoes

One of the tricks of light cooking is to substitute low-fat dairy products for ones that are higher in fat. Here, ricotta adds the creaminess that whipping cream normally would — and very deliciously, too!

Per serving: about
- 435 calories
- 18 g protein
- 11 g fat
- 66 g carbohydrate
- high source of fiber
- good source of calcium and iron

1 tbsp	olive oil	15 mL
1	onion, chopped	1
2	cloves garlic, minced	2
1	can (28 oz/796 mL) tomatoes	1
1/4 tsp	hot pepper flakes	1 mL
1/2 cup	chopped fresh parsley	125 mL
2 tbsp	chopped fresh oregano (or 2 tsp/10 mL dried)	25 mL
1 cup	ricotta cheese	250 mL
1/4 cup	2% milk	50 mL
5 cups	penne (1 lb/500 g)	1.25 L
	Salt and pepper	
1/4 cup	freshly grated Parmesan cheese	50 mL

● In heavy saucepan, heat oil over medium heat; cook onion and garlic, stirring occasionally, for 3 minutes.

● In food processor or blender, purée tomatoes; add to saucepan along with hot pepper flakes. Bring to boil; reduce heat and simmer, uncovered, for 20 minutes or until thickened. Add parsley and oregano; remove from heat.

● In food processor or blender, purée ricotta with milk until smooth. Stir into tomato mixture.

● Meanwhile, in large pot of boiling salted water, cook penne for 8 to 10 minutes or until tender but firm. Drain well and return to pot. Add sauce, and salt and pepper to taste; toss to coat. Serve sprinkled with Parmesan cheese. Makes 6 servings.

PASTA ON THE READY

With a variety of pastas, pot-ready pasta sauces, store-bought or your own pesto, cans of tuna and light versions of creamy and hard cheeses, you can face almost any dinner rush hour and end-of-the-month budget crisis. Smoked lean meats such as turkey, chicken or ham add a lot of flavor for not much cost and are worth stocking in the freezer, along with a variety of frozen vegetables.

Pasta Carbonara ▼

12	dry-packed sun-dried tomatoes (optional)	12
1 tbsp	olive oil	15 mL
1	clove garlic, minced	1
1	onion, chopped	1
3 cups	sliced mushrooms (8 oz/250 g)	750 mL
Half	sweet green pepper, chopped	Half
3/4 cup	diced lean ham or smoked turkey (4 oz/125 g)	175 mL
2	eggs	2
2	egg whites	2
1/2 cup	chicken stock	125 mL
12 oz	spaghettini	375 g
1/2 cup	freshly grated Parmesan cheese	125 mL
1/2 cup	chopped green onions or chives	125 mL
	Salt and pepper	

● In bowl, cover sun-dried tomatoes (if using) with boiling water; let stand for 8 to 10 minutes or until softened. Drain, chop and set aside.

● In skillet, heat oil over medium heat; cook garlic and onion, stirring occasionally, for 3 minutes or until fragrant.

● Add mushrooms and green pepper; cook over medium-high heat, stirring often, for 3 minutes or until softened and most of the moisture is evaporated. Add ham and sun-dried tomatoes; remove from heat.

● Beat together eggs, egg whites and stock; set aside.

● Meanwhile, in large pot of boiling salted water, cook spaghettini for 8 to 10 minutes or until tender but firm. Drain and return to pot. Add egg and vegetable mixtures; toss well over low heat for 2 minutes or until heated through. Remove from heat. Add Parmesan cheese, green onions, and salt and pepper to taste; toss to combine. Makes 4 servings.

I*t's a one-pot bonus when a pasta dish contains a vegetable-rich sauce, as this traditional delight does. For a more than satisfying supper, just add a salad and the proverbial crusty rolls.*

Per serving: about
- 520 calories
- 13 g fat
- good source of calcium and iron
- 28 g protein
- 71 g carbohydrate
- high source of fiber

Cheesy Vegetable Spirals

Pot-ready and quick-cooking, frozen mixed vegetables are a godsend when it comes to weekday meal preparation.

Per serving: about
- 785 calories
- 22 g fat
- very high source of fiber
- 38 g protein
- 112 g carbohydrate
- excellent source of calcium and iron

6 cups	rotini (12 oz/375 g)	1.5 L
6 cups	frozen mixed vegetables	1.5 L
2 cups	shredded Cheddar cheese (8 oz/250 g)	500 mL
1 cup	2% evaporated milk	250 mL
1	can (14 oz/398 mL) tomato sauce	1
1/2 tsp	dry mustard	2 mL
1/4 tsp	pepper	1 mL
1/4 cup	chopped fresh parsley	50 mL

● In large pot of boiling salted water, cook pasta for 8 to 10 minutes or until tender but firm. Add frozen vegetables; cook for 1 minute. Drain well and return to pot.

● Meanwhile, in saucepan, stir together 1-3/4 cups (425 mL) of the cheese, milk, tomato sauce, mustard and pepper; cook over medium heat, stirring often, for about 5 minutes or until cheese is melted.

● Add sauce to pasta mixture and toss to coat. Serve sprinkled with remaining cheese and parsley. Makes 4 servings.

Tomato Clam Linguine

With some cans of tomato sauce and baby clams on hand, it's always easy to whip up this delicious pasta dish.

Per serving: about
- 480 calories
- 9 g fat
- very high source of fiber
- 20 g protein
- 80 g carbohydrate
- excellent source of iron

2 tbsp	vegetable oil	25 mL
2	cloves garlic, minced	2
2	onions, chopped	2
1	can (10 oz/284 mL) baby clams	1
1	can (14 oz/398 mL) tomato sauce	1
1/4 cup	chopped fresh parsley	50 mL
2 tsp	granulated sugar	10 mL
1/4 tsp	each salt and pepper	1 mL
12 oz	linguine	375 g

● In large skillet, heat oil over medium heat; cook garlic and onions, stirring occasionally, for 5 minutes or until softened.

● Drain clams, reserving 1/3 cup (75 mL) juice. Add juice to skillet along with tomato sauce, half of the parsley, the sugar, salt and pepper; cook, uncovered, for 5 minutes or until slightly thickened. Add clams; cook for 1 minute.

● Meanwhile, in large pot of boiling salted water, cook pasta for 8 to 10 minutes or until tender but firm; drain well and return to pot. Add sauce; toss to coat. Serve sprinkled with remaining parsley. Makes 4 servings.

Stove-Top Tuna Casserole

To the rescue at a moment's notice — a dish with a tried-and-true record of pleasing generations of families, streamlined for today's busy times.

Per serving: about
- 535 calories
- 17 g fat
- high source of fiber
- 35 g protein
- 59 g carbohydrate
- good source of calcium and iron

6 cups	broad egg noodles	1.5 L
4 cups	frozen Oriental mixed vegetables	1 L
2 cups	milk	500 mL
1	pkg (250 g) light cream cheese, cubed	1
1 tsp	dried dillweed	5 mL
2	cans (each 6.5 oz/184 g) water-packed flaked light tuna, drained	2
1/2 tsp	salt	2 mL
1/4 tsp	pepper	1 mL

● In large pot of boiling salted water, cook noodles for 8 minutes or until tender but firm. Add vegetables; drain well and return to pot.

● Meanwhile, in saucepan, heat milk and cheese over medium heat, stirring, for 7 minutes or until cheese is melted. Stir in dill.

● Add sauce to noodles along with tuna; cook, stirring, over medium heat until piping hot. Season with salt and pepper. Makes 5 servings.

Chili Macaroni

1 tbsp	vegetable oil	15 mL
1	onion, chopped	1
1	sweet green pepper, chopped	1
2	cloves garlic, minced	2
1 lb	lean ground beef	500 g
1	can (19 oz/540 mL) kidney beans, drained and rinsed	1
1	can (14 oz/398 mL) tomato sauce	1
1 tbsp	chili powder	15 mL
1/4 tsp	pepper	1 mL
2 cups	macaroni	500 mL
1/2 cup	light sour cream or thick plain yogurt	125 mL

● In skillet, heat oil over medium heat; cook onion, green pepper and garlic, stirring occasionally, for 5 minutes or until softened.

● Add beef; cook over medium-high heat, breaking up with spoon, for 5 minutes or until no longer pink. Spoon off fat.

● Add kidney beans, tomato sauce, chili powder and pepper; cook for 3 minutes or until piping hot.

● Meanwhile, in large pot of boiling salted water, cook macaroni for 8 to 10 minutes or until tender but firm; drain well and return to pot. Add sauce; toss to coat. Serve topped with sour cream. Makes 4 servings.

Cross chili with pasta and what do you get? A kid-pleaser of a dish that will win over adults, too. You can even add some crunch appeal by crumbling corn chips over the top.

Per serving: about
- 610 calories
- 17 g fat
- very high source of fiber
- 39 g protein
- 76 g carbohydrate
- excellent source of iron

Pizza Spaghetti

2 tbsp	vegetable oil	25 mL
1	onion, chopped	1
1-1/4 cups	sliced mushrooms	300 mL
1 cup	sliced pepperoni	250 mL
1	sweet green pepper, chopped	1
1-1/2 tsp	dried oregano	7 mL
1	can (14 oz/398 mL) tomato sauce	1
1/4 tsp	each salt and pepper	1 mL
12 oz	spaghetti	375 g

● In skillet, heat oil over medium heat; cook onion, mushrooms, pepperoni, green pepper and oregano, stirring often, for 5 minutes or until onion is softened. Add tomato sauce, salt and pepper; cook for 3 minutes or until boiling.

● Meanwhile, in large pot of boiling salted water, cook spaghetti for 8 to 10 minutes or until tender but firm; drain well and return to pot. Add sauce; toss to coat. Makes 4 servings.

The next time the craving for pizza strikes, try this tomato-and-pepperoni sauce on a fast bowl of spaghetti, instead.

Per serving: about
- 605 calories
- 24 g fat
- very high source of fiber
- 20 g protein
- 77 g carbohydrate
- good source of iron

PASTA PRIMER

How much?
● As a main course, count on 4 oz (125 g) pasta per generous serving.

Which pasta?
Pairing the sauce to the shape ensures the sauce will coat the pasta evenly and makes the dish easier to eat.
● For long noodles such as spaghetti, lean to tomato and pesto sauces; the wider linguine and fettuccine take to mushrooms and soft vegetables. Use a creamy sauce if these noodles are fresh.
● Match stubby dried pastas, such as gemelli, penne and rigatoni, with chunky tomato sauces.
● A sauce with lentils, chick-peas or beans is perfect for conchiglie, farfalle, lumache, gnocchi or other pastas with hollows.

How to cook?
● Pasta needs lots of salted boiling water — at least 16 cups (4 L) per lb (500 g) of pasta. Begin tasting at least 1 minute before recommended time on package. Pasta should be firm but not hard.
● Drain in collander, saving some cooking water to thin sauce, if needed. Don't rinse — it cools the pasta and prevents the sauce from clinging.

Fusilli with Zucchini and Herbs

Cooking the onion slowly to release its flavor and using the chicken stock-based liquid to moisten mean less oil is required and the fat content remains moderate. You can substitute any corkscrew-shaped pasta for fusilli.

Per serving: about
- 480 calories
- 15 g protein
- 14 g fat
- 72 g carbohydrate
- high source of fiber

3 tbsp	olive oil	45 mL
1 tbsp	balsamic or red wine vinegar	15 mL
1	large onion, thinly sliced	1
3	small zucchini (1 lb/500 g total)	3
1/4 tsp	salt	1 mL
Pinch	pepper	Pinch
1/2 cup	chicken stock	125 mL
4 cups	fusilli (12 oz/375 g)	1 L
1/4 cup	chopped fresh mint (or 1/2 tsp/2 mL dried)	50 mL
2 tsp	chopped fresh mint (or 1/2 tsp/2 mL dried)	10 mL
1/4 cup	freshly grated Pecorino Romano or Parmesan cheese	50 mL

● In skillet, heat oil and vinegar over medium-high heat; cook onion, stirring occasionally, for about 15 minutes or until onion is very soft.

● Meanwhile, trim zucchini and cut in half lengthwise. Cut each half lengthwise into 1-inch (2.5 cm) pieces. Add to skillet along with salt and pepper; cook over medium-high heat, stirring often, for 7 to 10 minutes or until softened and turning golden. Pour in chicken stock; bring to boil, stirring to scrape up any brown bits.

● Meanwhile, in large pot of boiling salted water, cook fusilli for 8 to 10 minutes or until tender but firm. Drain well and return to pot, reserving 1/4 cup (50 mL) of the cooking liquid.

● Add zucchini mixture, basil and mint; toss gently, adding reserved liquid if necessary to moisten. Serve sprinkled with cheese. Makes 4 servings.

Rotelle with Beans and Prosciutto

While we suggest lima beans in this recipe, cooked red kidney beans or chopped fresh green beans are a convenient substitute. Add green beans to pasta for only the last 4 minutes of cooking. As for the kidney beans, sauté them up with the onion.

Per serving: about
- 475 calories
- 21 g protein
- 17 g fat
- 62 g carbohydrate
- excellent source of fiber and iron

4 cups	rotelle pasta (12 oz/375 g)	1 L
2 cups	frozen lima beans	500 mL
2 tbsp	olive oil	25 mL
2 tbsp	butter	25 mL
1	onion, chopped	1
4	cloves garlic, minced	4
1/4 tsp	hot pepper flakes	1 mL
1 cup	chicken stock	250 mL
1 tbsp	white wine vinegar	15 mL
3/4 tsp	salt	4 mL
3 cups	chopped Swiss chard or spinach	750 mL
4 oz	prosciutto or Black Forest ham, cut into strips	125 g
1/4 cup	chopped fresh oregano or parsley	50 mL

● In large pot of boiling salted water, cook pasta for 2 minutes. Add lima beans; cook for about 10 minutes or until pasta and beans are tender but firm. Drain well and return to pot.

● Meanwhile, in large skillet, heat oil with butter over medium heat; cook onion, garlic and hot pepper flakes, stirring occasionally, for about 5 minutes or until softened.

● Add stock, vinegar and salt; bring to boil. Add Swiss chard; toss for about 30 seconds or until wilted. Pour over pasta mixture. Add prosciutto and oregano; toss to coat. Makes 4 servings.

Tomato and Broccoli Pasta Toss ▲

4 cups	gemelli or rotini pasta (12 oz/375 g)	1 L
3 cups	small broccoli florets	750 mL
2 tbsp	olive oil	25 mL
1	sweet yellow pepper, chopped	1
1	onion, chopped	1
4	cloves garlic, minced	4
1 tsp	salt	5 mL
1/2 tsp	each pepper and granulated sugar	2 mL
4	large tomatoes, chopped	4
1/3 cup	shredded fresh basil	75 mL
1/4 cup	freshly grated Pecorino Romano or Parmesan cheese	50 mL

● In large pot of boiling salted water, cook pasta for 6 minutes. Add broccoli; cook for 2 to 3 minutes or until pasta is tender but firm and broccoli is tender-crisp. Drain, reserving 1/4 cup (50 mL) of the cooking liquid; return pasta mixture to pot.

● Meanwhile, in large skillet, heat oil over medium heat; cook yellow pepper, onion and garlic for 5 to 7 minutes or until onion is softened. Stir in reserved liquid, salt, pepper and sugar; bring to boil. Pour over pasta mixture. Add tomatoes, basil and cheese; toss to coat. Makes 4 servings.

Gemelli *means "twins" in Italian, hence the name for this pasta made from two short strands of spaghetti twisted together. Pronto means "right away," and that's how little time it takes to put this pasta on the table.*

Per serving: about
- 345 calories
- 10 g fat
- excellent source of fiber
- 12 g protein
- 54 g carbohydrate
- good source of iron

Main-Dish Salads

In the age of fajitas, stir-fries and burgers, it doesn't take a leap of faith to call a salad supper. Enjoy this selection of cold and grilled salad combos, which are blessedly long on flavor and short on prep time.

Turkey Pasta Salad with Thai Dressing ▶

Canadian Living's nutrition editor, Anne Lindsay, uses cooked turkey in this lunch or buffet dish, but cooked chicken would be just as delicious.

Per serving: about
- 340 calories
- 28 g protein
- 10 g fat
- 35 g carbohydrate
- good source of iron

2-1/2 cups	penne	625 mL
3 cups	cubed cooked turkey	750 mL
2 cups	coarsely shredded fresh spinach	500 mL
1 cup	julienned carrots	250 mL
1 cup	coarsely shredded red cabbage	250 mL
1/4 cup	chopped fresh coriander or parsley	50 mL
	THAI DRESSING	
1/4 cup	unsalted peanuts	50 mL
2 tbsp	minced gingerroot	25 mL
1/4 cup	lemon juice	50 mL
2 tbsp	low-sodium soy sauce	25 mL
1 tbsp	sesame oil	15 mL
1/4 tsp	hot pepper sauce	1 mL
1/4 tsp	each salt and pepper	1 mL

● In large pot of boiling salted water, cook pasta for 8 to 10 minutes or until tender but firm. Drain and rinse under cold water; drain again. In salad bowl, toss together pasta, turkey, spinach, carrots, cabbage and coriander.

● THAI DRESSING: In food processor or blender, chop peanuts and ginger finely. Add lemon juice, 1/4 cup (50 mL) water, soy sauce, sesame oil, hot pepper sauce, salt and pepper; combine well.

● Pour dressing over turkey mixture. Sprinkle with salt and pepper; toss to coat. Makes 6 servings.

TIP: To julienne carrots, cut into 2-inch (5 cm) lengths, then slice into matchstick-size strips.

THAI FLAVORS

Whenever a new ethnic or flavor trend shows up in restaurants, home cooks want to duplicate dishes almost immediately in their own kitchens. Yet it sometimes takes a while for ingredients to show up, especially in supermarkets.

● Thai is the latest trend in eating out, and by now many Chinese and Southeast Asian grocery stores, especially in larger cities, have the fresh lemongrass, Thai basil, mints and coriander, tiny hot peppers, galingal, fish sauce, coconut milk, rice-paper wrappers and curry mixes that deliver authentic flavors.

● In a pinch, substitutes can be made — fresh gingerroot can replace galingal, lemon rind the lemongrass and soy sauce the fish sauce; a mix of fresh parsley and dried cilantro (the Spanish name for coriander) can take over from fresh coriander. The dishes made with these substitutions won't have exactly the same taste as the original recipe, but they will still taste good.

Chicken and Pesto Pasta Salad

Both pasta and chicken are resplendent in a vibrant pesto sauce. While quick and easy enough for every day, this warm grilled salad can also be company fare, especially when fresh basil is greening the herb patch.

Per serving: about
- 635 calories
- 23 g fat
- high source of fiber
- 41 g protein
- 67 g carbohydrate
- good source of iron

1 lb	boneless skinless chicken breasts	500 g
4 cups	rotini (12 oz/375 g)	1 L
1/4 cup	toasted pine nuts	50 mL
2 tbsp	freshly grated Parmesan cheese	25 mL
	Lettuce leaves or mixed greens	
1/4 cup	shredded fresh basil	50 mL
	PESTO DRESSING	
2 cups	packed fresh basil leaves	500 mL
2	cloves garlic, quartered	2
1/4 cup	olive oil	50 mL
2 tbsp	white wine vinegar	25 mL
1/2 tsp	each salt and pepper	2 mL

● PESTO DRESSING: In food processor, finely chop basil with garlic. With motor running, gradually add oil, vinegar, salt and pepper until smooth.

● Place chicken in glass dish just big enough to hold in single layer. Remove 1 tbsp (15 mL) of the dressing; brush all over chicken. Cover and let stand at room temperature for 30 minutes.

● Meanwhile, in large pot of boiling salted water, cook rotini for 8 to 10 minutes or until tender but firm. Drain well, reserving 1/4 cup (50 mL) cooking liquid. Place pasta in large bowl. Add dressing and reserved cooking liquid; toss well. Stir in pine nuts and cheese.

● Meanwhile, place chicken on greased grill over medium-high heat; close lid and cook, turning once, for about 10 minutes or until chicken is no longer pink inside. Slice crosswise into thin strips.

● Mound pasta on lettuce-lined plates; top with chicken strips. Sprinkle with basil. Makes 4 servings.

Tomato-Corn Pasta Salad

This light vegetarian supper salad features flavorful feta cheese plus fiber-rich beans and corn.

Per serving: about
- 380 calories
- 9 g fat
- very high source of fiber
- 15 g protein
- 63 g carbohydrate
- good source of iron

5 cups	penne (1 lb/500 g)	1.25 L
5	tomatoes (2 lb/1 kg), seeded and cut into chunks	5
2 tbsp	olive oil	25 mL
2 tbsp	lemon juice	25 mL
2	cloves garlic, minced	2
1 tsp	salt	5 mL
1/4 tsp	pepper	1 mL
1 cup	cooked corn kernels	250 mL
1 cup	crumbled feta cheese	250 mL
1 cup	chopped fresh parsley	250 mL
1	can (19 oz/540 mL) kidney beans, drained and rinsed	1
1/2 cup	finely chopped fresh coriander	125 mL

● In large pot of boiling salted water, cook penne for 8 to 10 minutes or until tender but firm. Drain well and rinse under cold water; drain again.

● Meanwhile, in large bowl, combine tomatoes, oil, lemon juice, 1/4 cup (50 mL) water, garlic, salt and pepper; let stand for 5 minutes.

● Add pasta, corn, feta cheese, parsley, kidney beans and coriander; toss to combine. Makes 8 servings.

TIP: Fresh coriander, also known as cilantro, is a delight to some palates, less savory to others. Replace it with fresh basil, if desired.

Creamy Herbed Pasta Salad ▲

6 cups	fusilli or other short pasta (12 oz/375 g)	1.5 L
1	sweet red pepper	1
3	green onions	3
1 cup	firmly packed fresh basil leaves	250 mL
1/2 cup	fresh parsley leaves	125 mL
1/4 cup	freshly grated Parmesan cheese	50 mL
1	tub (500 g) 2% cottage cheese	1
1 tbsp	lemon juice	15 mL
1 tbsp	Dijon mustard	15 mL
1/2 tsp	pepper	2 mL
1/3 cup	vegetable or chicken stock	75 mL
1	can (19 oz/540 mL) red kidney beans, drained and rinsed	1

● In large pot of boiling salted water, cook fusilli for 8 to 10 minutes or until tender but firm; drain well.

● Meanwhile, cut red pepper into 1-inch (2.5 cm) long strips; dice enough to make 1/4 cup (50 mL). Chop green onions. Set aside.

● In food processor, finely mince together basil, parsley and Parmesan cheese. Add cottage cheese, lemon juice, mustard and pepper; purée for 20 seconds or until smooth. Add stock; mix well.

● In large bowl, toss together pasta, red pepper strips, green onions, kidney beans and sauce until coated. Serve garnished with diced red pepper. Makes 4 servings.

Humans that we are, we eat with our eyes first. And what a visual enticement this vegetarian main-course salad is — curly pasta, rich red kidney beans and diced red peppers and onions.

Per serving: about
- 595 calories
- 7 g fat
- very high source of fiber
- excellent source of iron
- 40 g protein
- 92 g carbohydrate
- good source of calcium

Chick-Pea, Orange and Watercress Salad ◄

1	orange	1
1 cup	rinsed drained chick-peas	250 mL
1/4 cup	chopped red onion	50 mL
2 tbsp	chopped fresh mint	25 mL
1/4 cup	orange juice	50 mL
1 tsp	red wine vinegar	5 mL
1 tsp	sesame oil	5 mL
1/2 tsp	grated gingerroot	2 mL
1	bunch watercress or arugula, coarse stems removed	1

● Peel orange. Holding orange over bowl to catch juices, cut off outer white membrane; cut between sections and membranes to remove sections. Add sections to bowl. Add chick-peas, onion and mint.

● Whisk together orange juice, vinegar, oil and ginger; pour over chick-pea mixture and toss to combine.

● Arrange watercress on small serving platter. Spoon chick-pea mixture over top. Makes 4 servings.

This low-fat, calorie-wise salad is a powerhouse of nutrients. It will provide 63 per cent of your daily requirement for vitamin C and 20 per cent of your daily need for folate, a B vitamin.

Per serving: about
- 105 calories
- 5 g protein
- 2 g fat
- 18 g carbohydrate

Grilled Vegetable and Couscous Salad

2	small zucchini	2
1	eggplant	1
1	each sweet red and yellow pepper	1
1	red onion	1
1/4 cup	olive oil	50 mL
1/4 cup	coarsely chopped black olives	50 mL
1/2 tsp	salt	2 mL
1 cup	couscous (preferably whole wheat)	250 mL
	DRESSING	
1/4 cup	olive oil	50 mL
1 tbsp	white wine vinegar	15 mL
1	plum tomato, finely diced	1
2	cloves garlic, minced	2
1 tsp	each dried thyme, oregano and basil	5 mL
1/2 tsp	each salt and pepper	2 mL

● DRESSING: In small bowl, whisk together oil, vinegar, tomato, garlic, thyme, oregano, basil, salt and pepper. Set aside.

● Slice zucchini and eggplant into 1/2-inch (1 cm) thick slices. Cut red and yellow peppers into quarters. Cut onion crosswise into 1/2-inch (1 cm) thick slices. Brush vegetables all over with oil.

● Place vegetables on greased grill over medium-high heat, in batches if necessary; close lid and cook, turning often, for 7 to 10 minutes or until eggplant, zucchini and onion are softened but not charred and peppers are tender-crisp. Cut into generous bite-size pieces; place in large bowl. Add dressing and black olives; toss to coat.

● Meanwhile, in small saucepan, bring 1-1/4 cups (300 mL) water and salt to boil; stir in couscous. Remove from heat; cover and let stand for 5 minutes. Fluff with fork and add to bowl; toss to combine. Makes 4 servings.

Grilling enhances the flavor of almost everything, including vegetables — and most impressively, too. Here, summer zucchini, eggplant, vivid peppers and red onion make an unforgettable salad tossed with couscous. This combination takes well to a crumble of feta cheese, so please indulge if you like.

Per serving: about
- 525 calories
- 9 g protein
- 29 g fat
- 60 g carbohydrate
- high source of fiber
- good source of iron

TIP: When you're looking for olives with the most flavor, opt for black ones. As the availability of different kinds of black olives improves, especially in areas where Italians, Greeks or Portuguese have made their homes, you can find infornata, gaeta or Kalamata — each one a guarantee of lots of olive flavor for your money! Avoid the blander canned black olives.

Grilled Portobellinis on Bean Salad

One of the most delicious new choices in mushrooms is the portobello, or its smaller version, the portobellini — a mature and flavorful fungus that takes to the grill fabulously. On a salad of beans with biting arugula and sweet pepper, it's vegetarian eating at its finest.

Per serving: about
- 425 calories
- 23 g fat
- very high source of fiber
- excellent source of iron
- 17 g protein
- 43 g carbohydrate
- good source of calcium

8	portobellini or small portobello mushrooms (12 oz/375 g)	8
1	can (19 oz/540 mL) white pea beans, drained and rinsed	1
2/3 cup	chopped celery	150 mL
1/4 cup	finely chopped red onion	50 mL
Half	small sweet red pepper, chopped	Half
2 tbsp	chopped fresh parsley	25 mL
1	bunch arugula or watercress, coarse stems removed	1
1 oz	Asiago or Parmesan cheese, shaved	30 g
	DRESSING	
1/4 cup	olive oil	50 mL
3 tbsp	white wine vinegar	50 mL
1 tbsp	chopped fresh rosemary or thyme	15 mL
2	cloves garlic, minced	2
1/4 tsp	each salt and pepper	1 mL

● DRESSING: In small bowl, whisk together oil, vinegar, rosemary, garlic, salt and pepper.

● Cut stems off mushrooms just below cap and reserve for another use. Wipe top of caps with damp towel. Remove 1 tbsp (15 mL) of the dressing; brush over mushrooms. Place on greased grill over medium-high heat; close lid and cook, turning once, for 8 to 10 minutes or until tender. Slice if desired.

● Meanwhile, in large bowl, toss together pea beans, celery, onion, red pepper, parsley and remaining dressing to coat.

● Line plates with arugula; mound bean salad on top. Place 2 or 3 mushrooms on each salad. Top with cheese. Serve immediately. Makes 3 servings.

Broccoli and Mushroom Salad

When Canadian Living celebrated its twentieth anniversary, we opened our pages to recipes from readers — including this one from Janet Mather of Toronto, who wrote that two of her daughters love this salad so much "they actually beg for it in their school lunches."

Per serving: about
- 300 calories
- 25 g fat
- good source of iron
- 6 g protein
- 16 g carbohydrate

1/2 cup	sliced or slivered almonds	125 mL
2 tbsp	sesame seeds	25 mL
1	stalk broccoli, chopped	1
12 oz	bean sprouts	375 g
2 cups	sliced mushrooms (6 oz/175 g)	500 mL
2	green onions, chopped	2
1/4 cup	sunflower seeds	50 mL
2 cups	chow mein noodles	500 mL
	DRESSING	
1/2 cup	vegetable oil	125 mL
3 tbsp	rice vinegar	45 mL
2 tbsp	light soy sauce	25 mL
1 tbsp	granulated sugar	15 mL
1-1/2 tsp	sesame oil	7 mL
1	clove garlic, minced	1
1/2 tsp	pepper	2 mL
	Salt	

● In skillet, toast almonds and sesame seeds over medium heat, stirring occasionally, for about 8 minutes or until fragrant. Set aside.

● In large bowl, combine broccoli, bean sprouts, mushrooms, onions and sunflower seeds. Add toasted almonds and sesame seeds. *(Salad can be prepared to this point, covered and refrigerated for up to 4 hours.)*

● DRESSING: In small bowl, whisk together vegetable oil, vinegar, soy sauce, sugar, sesame oil, garlic, pepper, and salt to taste. *(Dressing can be covered and refrigerated for up to 4 hours.)*

● Add dressing to broccoli mixture; toss to coat. Sprinkle with chow mein noodles. Makes 8 servings.

Steak and Mushroom Salad ▲

2 tbsp	red wine vinegar	25 mL
2 tbsp	vegetable oil	25 mL
1/2 tsp	Dijon mustard	2 mL
2 tbsp	teriyaki sauce	25 mL
8 oz	lean steak, trimmed	250 g
1/2 tsp	pepper	2 mL
3/4 cup	sliced mushrooms	175 mL
1/2 cup	beef stock	125 mL
2 tbsp	red wine or red wine vinegar	25 mL
4 cups	torn salad greens	1 L

● Whisk together vinegar, oil and mustard; reserve half, covered. Combine remainder in large shallow dish with teriyaki sauce. Add steak, turning to coat. Cover and marinate in refrigerator for at least 3 hours or for up to 12 hours.

● Brush marinade off steak and reserve. In greased nonstick skillet, brown steak over high heat, turning once, for 2 minutes. Reduce heat to medium-high; cook, turning once, for 6 minutes for rare or until desired doneness. Transfer to plate and season with pepper; tent with foil.

● Add mushrooms to pan; cook, stirring, for 1 minute. Stir in reserved marinade from meat, stock and wine; cook for 2 to 3 minutes or until slightly reduced.

● Meanwhile, toss greens with remaining vinegar mixture; arrange on plates. Thinly slice steak; arrange over greens. Spoon mushroom mixture over top. Makes 2 servings.

*Y*ou don't need a lot of steak to toss up this satisfying year-round salad. We recommend sirloin for the steak, and a contrasting mix of greens and red-tinged lettuces — such as red romaine, Bibb, spinach and watercress — to give this meal-in-a-bowl extra eye appeal.

Per serving: about
- 320 calories
- 19 g fat
- excellent source of iron
- 29 g protein
- 8 g carbohydrate

Chicken Potato Salad ▲

Cube leftover roast or grilled chicken or even turkey, for a colorful one-bowl salad supper. Try it on a bed of cucumber and lettuce.

Per serving: about
- 230 calories
- 6 g fat
- 20 g protein
- 26 g carbohydrate

2 lb	new red potatoes (unpeeled)	1 kg
3 cups	cubed cooked chicken	750 mL
1 cup	cooked corn kernels	250 mL
1	sweet red pepper, chopped	1
4	green onions, sliced	4
	Fresh basil sprigs	
	DRESSING	
1/4 cup	chopped fresh basil	50 mL
3 tbsp	cider vinegar	50 mL
1/2 tsp	each salt, pepper and granulated sugar	2 mL
2 tbsp	vegetable oil	25 mL
1/4 cup	light sour cream	50 mL

● DRESSING: In small bowl, whisk together basil, vinegar, salt, pepper and sugar; gradually whisk in oil. Gradually whisk in sour cream and 1 tbsp (15 mL) water. *(Dressing can be covered and refrigerated for up to 6 hours.)*

● Quarter or halve potatoes. In pot of lightly salted boiling water, cook potatoes for about 20 minutes or until tender; drain and let cool completely.

● Cut potatoes into bite-size chunks and transfer to large serving bowl; add chicken, corn, red pepper and onions, stirring to combine. *(Salad can be prepared to this point, covered and refrigerated for up to 6 hours.)*

● Pour dressing over salad; toss gently to combine. Garnish with basil sprigs. Makes 4 servings.

Crunchy Vegetable and Lentil Salad

2	cans (each 19 oz/540 mL) lentils or black beans, drained and rinsed	2
2	sweet red peppers, chopped	2
2 cups	cooked corn kernels	500 mL
1 cup	chopped celery	250 mL
1 cup	cubed light Jarlsberg-style cheese	250 mL
1/2 cup	chopped green onions	125 mL
1/4 cup	chopped fresh coriander	50 mL
1/3 cup	cider vinegar	75 mL
1 tbsp	water	15 mL
1 tbsp	Dijon mustard	15 mL
1/2 tsp	each salt and pepper	2 mL
1/4 cup	vegetable oil	50 mL

● In bowl, combine lentils, red peppers, corn, celery, cheese, onions and coriander.

● In a separate bowl, whisk together vinegar, water, mustard, salt and pepper; gradually whisk in oil. Pour over salad, stirring to coat. *(Salad can be covered and refrigerated for up to 1 day.)* Makes 4 servings.

Look for one of the lighter cheeses to complement this flavorful fiber-rich salad. Serve it in Boston or romaine lettuce leaves with whole-wheat rolls or bread.

Per serving: about
- 530 calories
- 20 g fat
- very high source of fiber
- excellent source of iron
- 30 g protein
- 65 g carbohydrate
- excellent source of calcium

TIP: To cook your own lentils, choose large green or brown lentils and boil in lightly salted water for about 30 minutes or until tender. Drain well. For 2 cups (500 mL) cooked lentils (the yield from a 19 oz/540 mL can), start with 1 cup (250 mL) dried.

Beef and Vegetable Rice Salad

1-1/2 cups	long-grain rice	375 mL
1-1/2 cups	thinly sliced cooked beef (about 9 oz/275 g)	375 mL
1	sweet yellow or red pepper, chopped	1
1	carrot, chopped	1
1	small zucchini, chopped	1
1/4 cup	lemon juice	50 mL
2 tbsp	each chopped fresh oregano and mint	25 mL
2 tbsp	white wine vinegar	25 mL
2 tsp	Dijon mustard	10 mL
1/2 tsp	each salt and pepper	2 mL
1/4 cup	olive oil	50 mL
1 cup	trimmed watercress or shredded lettuce	250 mL

● In saucepan, bring 3 cups (750 mL) water to boil. Stir in rice; cover, reduce heat and simmer for 20 minutes or until liquid is absorbed and rice is tender. Fluff with fork. Transfer to bowl; let cool. Add beef, yellow pepper, carrot and zucchini.

● Whisk together lemon juice, oregano, mint, vinegar, mustard, salt and pepper; gradually whisk in oil. Pour over salad; stir to coat. Cover and refrigerate for at least 1 hour or for up to 24 hours. To serve, gently stir in watercress. Makes 4 servings.

Leftover grilled steak or roast beef is the inspiration for a speedy salad supper. Spoon it into lettuce cups or extra watercress and slice tomatoes to go alongside.

Per serving: about
- 540 calories
- 20 g fat
- good source of iron
- 26 g protein
- 62 g carbohydrate

TIP: Keep this salad in mind when planning packed lunches. Spoon the dressed salad into an airtight container and pack the watercress or lettuce separately to toss together just before enjoying.

Warm Sausage and Potato Salad ▼

Author and food writer Rose Murray lives in Waterloo County, Ontario, a region noted for its excellent sausages. Here's one of her deliciously satisfying country suppers — a blissful union of sausages, potato salad and green beans in a sweet-and-tangy mustard dressing. You can broil or pan-fry sausages.

Per serving: about
- 495 calories
- 27 g fat
- high source of fiber
- 21 g protein
- 42 g carbohydrate
- good source of iron

1-3/4 lb	new red potatoes	875 g
4 oz	green beans or sugar snap peas	125 g
Half	sweet red pepper	Half
1/2 cup	diced red onion	125 mL
1/4 cup	packed shredded fresh basil	50 mL
1 lb	sausage	500 g
	Lettuce leaves	
	SWEET MUSTARD DRESSING	
3 tbsp	each cider vinegar, chicken stock and olive oil	50 mL
4 tsp	sweet mustard	20 mL
1	clove garlic, minced	1
Dash	Worcestershire sauce	Dash
1/2 tsp	pepper	2 mL

● SWEET MUSTARD DRESSING: In small bowl, whisk together vinegar, stock, oil, mustard, garlic, Worcestershire sauce and pepper. Set aside.

● Scrub potatoes; halve or quarter if large. Trim beans; cut diagonally in half. Cut red pepper in half crosswise; cut lengthwise into strips. In saucepan of boiling salted water, cook potatoes for 15 minutes or just until fork-tender. Remove with slotted spoon and cut into 1-inch (2.5 cm) cubes; place in large bowl.

● Add beans to boiling water; cook for about 5 minutes or just until tender-crisp. Drain and cool under cold water; drain well and add to bowl. Pour in all but 2 tbsp (25 mL) of the dressing; gently stir in red pepper, onion and basil.

● Meanwhile, prick sausage and place on greased grill over medium-high heat; close lid and cook, turning often and brushing with remaining dressing, for 20 to 25 minutes or until no longer pink inside. Slice thickly on diagonal.

● Mound potato mixture on lettuce-lined plates; arrange sausage slices over top. Makes 4 servings.

TIP: When choosing sweet-and-tangy mustard, look for Russian or Russian-style. Avoid bright-yellow honey mustards, although one of the finest in the Russian-style mustards is called Honeycup.

Barley Supper Salad

3 cups	vegetable stock	750 mL
1 cup	pearl or pot barley	250 mL
1	bay leaf	1
2	carrots, chopped	2
2	stalks celery, chopped	2
4	green onions, chopped	4
Half	sweet green pepper, chopped	Half
1	can (19 oz/540 mL) red kidney beans, drained and rinsed	1
1/4 cup	chopped fresh parsley	50 mL
	Lettuce leaves	
	DRESSING	
1/4 cup	vegetable stock	50 mL
1/3 cup	red wine vinegar	75 mL
1 tbsp	Dijon mustard	15 mL
2 tsp	dried basil	10 mL
1 tsp	dried thyme	5 mL
1/3 cup	olive oil	75 mL

● In saucepan, combine stock, barley and bay leaf; bring to boil. Reduce heat, cover and simmer for 40 minutes.

● Stir in carrots and celery; cook for 5 minutes or until stock is absorbed and barley is tender. Discard bay leaf. Transfer to large bowl; fluff with fork. Add green onions, green pepper and kidney beans.

● DRESSING: In small bowl, whisk together stock, vinegar, mustard, basil and thyme; gradually whisk in oil.

● Add to barley mixture; toss to combine. Cover and refrigerate for at least 2 hours or for up to 8 hours. Stir in parsley. Serve on lettuce-lined plates. Makes 6 servings.

Barley takes a little longer to cook than our usual 30 minutes, but this fiber-rich grain can be made ahead and is a welcome break from rice, pasta and potatoes. You can find it wherever dry beans or lentils are sold.

Per serving: about
- 330 calories
- 13 g fat
- very high source of fiber
- 9 g protein
- 47 g carbohydrate
- good source of iron

Grilled Lamb on Tabbouleh

8	lamb loin chops	8
1/2 cup	fine bulgur	125 mL
3/4 cup	cubed (unpeeled) English cucumber	175 mL
1/2 cup	chopped fresh parsley	125 mL
2	green onions	2
1	large tomato, chopped	1
	Romaine lettuce leaves	
	DRESSING	
1/4 cup	chopped fresh mint (or 2 tsp/10 mL dried)	50 mL
3 tbsp	olive oil	45 mL
1 tsp	grated lemon rind	5 mL
3 tbsp	lemon juice	45 mL
1/2 tsp	each salt and pepper	2 mL

● DRESSING: In small bowl, whisk together mint, oil, lemon rind and juice, salt and pepper.

● Trim fat from lamb; slash edges. Place in glass dish just big enough to hold chops in single layer. Remove 1 tbsp (15 mL) of the dressing; spread over lamb. Let stand for 30 minutes at room temperature.

● Meanwhile, soak bulgur in 2 cups (500 mL) hot water for 30 minutes. Drain in fine sieve and transfer to large bowl; pour in remaining dressing. Add cucumber, parsley, onions and tomato; stir gently to combine.

● Place chops on greased grill over medium-high heat; close lid and cook, turning once, for about 10 minutes or until just pink inside.

● Line plates with lettuce; mound bulgur mixture over top. Top each with 2 chops. Makes 4 servings.

Enjoy this refreshing grilled salad plate with warmed pita breads. Opt for the broiler in cold weather.

Per serving : about
- 290 calories
- 16 g fat
- high source of fiber
- 21 g protein
- 19 g carbohydrate
- good source of iron

Satisfying Soups

Although most soups take more than 30 minutes to prepare, they need little tending and are easy to make-ahead. We've also included a selection of soups that have all the taste of hours in the pot, but come together surprisingly quickly.

Split Pea Simmer ▶

A ham hock packs the flavor needed for this large batch of soup, but a ham bone will do as well. If you have neither, simmer the peas with celery and herbs for 1 hour, then add about 12 oz (375 g) sliced smoked sausage or chunky ham.

Per serving: about
- 310 calories
- 3 g fat
- very high source of fiber
- 24 g protein
- 49 g carbohydrate
- good source of iron

4 cups	green split peas	1 L
1	smoked ham hock (2 lb/1 kg)	1
1	stalk celery (with leaves)	1
1	bay leaf	1
1/4 tsp	dried thyme	1 mL
2 cups	cubed peeled rutabaga	500 mL
1 cup	cubed celery root or celery	250 mL
2	carrots, chopped	2
1	onion, chopped	1
1	large potato, peeled and chopped	1
1-1/2 tsp	pepper	7 mL
	Salt	

● Rinse peas and ham hock; place in stock pot or large saucepan. Add 16 cups (4 L) water; bring to boil, skimming off foam.

● Add celery, bay leaf and thyme. Reduce heat, cover and simmer for 2 hours or until peas and meat on hock are tender, skimming off foam as necessary. Remove from heat.

● Discard celery and bay leaf. Remove ham hock; let cool. Pull off meat; discard bone, skin and fat. Cube meat; set aside. *(Soup and meat can be prepared to this point and refrigerated in separate airtight containers for up to 3 days.)* Skim fat from soup.

● In clean saucepan, combine split pea mixture, rutabaga, celery root, carrots, onion, potato and pepper; bring to boil.

● Reduce heat and simmer, stirring often, for 20 minutes or until vegetables are tender, adding up to 1 cup (250 mL) more water if soup is too thick.

● Return cubed ham to soup. Season with salt to taste. Makes 12 servings.

SOUP BASICS
● Good powdered stock and condensed or canned broth are reasonable substitutes for homemade stock. Low-sodium canned broth is a good choice when chicken broth is called for.
● Most soups are better for a last-minute addition of herbs. Even if herbs have been called for in the recipe, taste the soup before serving and punch up the flavor with more herbs if needed.

(Bottom) Split Pea Simmer; (top) Tortellini Soup (p. 81)

Black Bean Vegetable Soup ▲

This is one soup you don't have to make ahead to enjoy on a busy evening. Add a drizzle of guacamole and serve with a salad and rolls.

Per serving: about
- 180 calories
- 8 g protein
- 4 g fat
- 31 g carbohydrate
- very high source of fiber

1 tbsp	vegetable oil	15 mL
1	onion, chopped	1
1	clove garlic, minced	1
2	carrots, chopped	2
2 tsp	chili powder	10 mL
1 tsp	ground cumin	5 mL
4 cups	vegetable stock	1 L
2	cans (each 14 oz/398 mL) black beans, drained and rinsed	2
1	can (7 oz/199 mL) corn kernels	1
1/4 tsp	pepper	1 mL
1	can (10 oz/284 mL) stewed tomatoes	1

● In large heavy saucepan, heat oil over medium heat; cook onion, garlic and carrots, stirring occasionally, for 5 minutes or until onion is softened.

● Add chili powder and cumin; cook, stirring, for 1 minute. Add stock, 1 can of the beans, corn and pepper; bring to boil.

● Meanwhile, in food processor or blender, purée together tomatoes and remaining can of beans; add to pot. Reduce heat, cover and simmer for 10 to 15 minutes or until carrots are tender. Makes 6 servings.

Tortellini Soup

1 tbsp	vegetable oil	15 mL
1	onion, chopped	1
1	clove garlic, minced	1
2 cups	chopped carrots	500 mL
3/4 cup	sliced celery	175 mL
4 cups	chicken stock	1 L
1 tbsp	lemon juice	15 mL
1/2 tsp	each dried basil and thyme	2 mL
2 cups	cheese tortellini (about 7 oz/200 g)	500 mL
1/2 cup	frozen peas	125 mL
1/4 cup	(approx) freshly grated Parmesan cheese	50 mL
1/4 cup	sliced green onion tops or chopped fresh parsley	50 mL

● In heavy saucepan, heat oil over medium heat; cook onion, garlic, carrots and celery, stirring often, for about 5 minutes or until slightly softened.

● Add stock, lemon juice, basil and thyme; bring to boil. Reduce heat, cover and simmer for about 15 minutes or until carrots are tender.

● Add tortellini; bring to boil. Reduce heat and simmer, covered, for 5 minutes. Stir in peas and 1/4 cup (50 mL) Parmesan cheese; heat until steaming. Ladle into bowls. Sprinkle with green onion, and Parmesan cheese, if desired. Makes 4 servings.

Add cheese-filled tortellini, carrots and frozen peas to your shopping list and you can enjoy this quick-cooking soup any night of the week (photo, p.79).

Per serving: about
- 295 calories
- 10 g fat
- high source of fiber
- 16 g protein
- 36 g carbohydrate
- good source of calcium and iron

Smoky Squash and Tomato Soup

8 oz	smoked sausage, sliced	250 g
2	carrots, sliced	2
4 cups	chicken stock	1 L
1	can (28 oz/796 mL) tomatoes	1
1	large onion, chopped	1
2	stalks celery, chopped	2
2	cloves garlic, slivered	2
4 cups	diced peeled squash	1 L
1/2 tsp	thyme (or 2 tsp/10 mL dried)	2 mL
Pinch	hot pepper flakes	Pinch
1	can (19 oz/540 mL) chick-peas or red kidney beans, drained and rinsed	1
1/3 cup	chopped fresh parsley	75 mL
	Freshly grated Parmesan cheese	

● In large heavy saucepan, bring sausage, carrots and stock to boil; reduce heat, cover and simmer for 5 minutes or until carrots are tender.

● Add tomatoes, breaking up with spoon. Add onion, celery, garlic, squash, thyme and hot pepper flakes; bring to boil. Reduce heat and simmer, covered, for about 15 minutes or until vegetables are tender.

● Add chick-peas; simmer for 10 minutes. Ladle into bowls. Sprinkle with parsley, and Parmesan cheese to taste. Makes 8 servings.

Here's all the flavor of a long simmer in record time, thanks to smoky lean sausages and canned chick-peas. Be sure to include the celery leaves — they add their own great taste to any soup.

Per serving: about
- 225 calories
- 8 g fat
- high source of fiber
- 12 g protein
- 28 g carbohydrate
- good source of iron

Spicy Chicken Noodle Soup

Chicken soup goes Thai and trendy with the freshness of lime, the warm glow of turmeric, the heat of chili and the crunch of lettuce and sprouts.

Per serving: about
- 155 calories
- 15 g protein
- 2 g fat
- 18 g carbohydrate

8 oz	boneless skinless chicken breasts	250 g
4 oz	rice vermicelli noodles	125 g
3	cloves garlic, minced	3
1 tbsp	ground cumin	15 mL
1/2 tsp	turmeric	2 mL
5 cups	chicken stock	1.25 L
1/2 tsp	grated lime rind	2 mL
2 tbsp	lime juice	25 mL
2 tsp	chopped gingerroot or hot pepper sauce	10 mL
2 tsp	granulated sugar	10 mL
1 tsp	chili paste	5 mL
1 cup	bean sprouts	250 mL
1 cup	coarsely chopped romaine lettuce	250 mL
2 tbsp	chopped fresh coriander	25 mL

● Cut chicken into thin strips. Break noodles into 3-inch (8 cm) long pieces. Set aside.

● In large saucepan, combine garlic, cumin and turmeric; cook over medium heat, stirring constantly, for 1 minute.

● Add chicken, chicken stock, lime rind and juice, ginger, sugar and chili paste; bring to boil. Reduce heat and simmer for 5 minutes.

● Add noodles; simmer for 3 minutes. Add bean sprouts and lettuce; cook for 1 minute. Ladle into bowls. Sprinkle with coriander. Makes 6 servings.

Quick Pasta e Fagioli

In main-course pasta dishes, salads and in this delicious soup, pasta and beans are always a winning combo. Simmer a pot to warm up appetites on a cold winter's night, and serve with crusty bread and lightly dressed greens.

Per serving: about
- 250 calories
- 15 g protein
- 5 g fat
- 39 g carbohydrate
- very high source of fiber
- good source of iron

1 tbsp	olive oil	15 mL
1	onion, chopped	1
2	cloves garlic, minced	2
1	can (28 oz/796 mL) tomatoes	1
2	cans (each 19 oz/540 mL) white kidney beans, drained and rinsed	2
2 cups	vegetable stock	500 mL
1/4 cup	slivered sun-dried tomatoes	50 mL
1/2 tsp	each dried basil and oregano	2 mL
1/4 tsp	pepper	1 mL
1/2 cup	macaroni	125 mL
1/4 cup	freshly grated Parmesan cheese	50 mL

● In large heavy saucepan, heat oil over medium heat; cook onion and garlic, stirring, for 3 minutes.

● Add tomatoes, breaking up with spoon. Add beans, stock, sun-dried tomatoes, basil, oregano and pepper; bring to boil. Reduce heat, cover and simmer for 20 minutes.

● Stir in pasta; return to boil. Reduce heat and simmer, covered, for 10 minutes or until pasta is tender. Ladle into bowls. Sprinkle with Parmesan cheese. Makes 6 servings.

Carrot and Ham Soup

2 tsp	butter	10 mL
1	onion, chopped	1
3 cups	sliced carrots	750 mL
4 cups	chicken stock	1 L
1 cup	cubed cooked ham	250 mL
Pinch	dried thyme	Pinch
1/4 cup	long-grain rice	50 mL
2 tbsp	chopped fresh parsley	25 mL
1/4 tsp	salt	1 mL
	Pepper	

● In large heavy saucepan, melt butter over medium heat; cook onion and carrots, stirring occasionally, for about 5 minutes or until softened.

● Stir in stock, ham and thyme; bring to boil. Stir in rice. Reduce heat to medium-low; cover and simmer for 25 to 30 minutes or just until carrots and rice are tender. Stir in parsley and salt; season with pepper to taste. Makes 4 servings.

This soup is so easy, so inexpensive and, best of all, so good!

Per serving: about
- 205 calories
- 6 g fat
- 15 g protein
- 22 g carbohydrate

Broccoli Bean Soup

1 tbsp	vegetable oil	15 mL
1 cup	chopped onion	250 mL
2	cloves garlic, chopped	2
4 cups	coarsely chopped broccoli (about 1 bunch)	1 L
2-1/2 cups	chicken stock	625 mL
1	potato, peeled and diced	1
1 cup	drained canned white pea (navy) beans	250 mL
1-1/2 cups	shredded light Cheddar-style cheese	375 mL
1 cup	1% milk	250 mL
1/4 tsp	each salt and pepper	1 mL

● In large heavy saucepan, heat oil over medium heat; cook onion and garlic, stirring occasionally, for 3 minutes or until softened.

● Add broccoli, stock, potato and beans; bring to boil. Reduce heat, cover and simmer for about 20 minutes or until softened.

● In food processor or blender, purée vegetable mixture to desired consistency; return to saucepan. Stir in half of the cheese. Add milk, salt and pepper; cook over medium-low heat, stirring, just until cheese is melted. Ladle into bowls. Sprinkle with remaining cheese. Makes 6 servings.

Perfect for chilly weather, this full-flavored soup is loaded with calcium from broccoli, beans, milk and cheese. For a non-dairy version, omit the cheese and milk and use water to thin the soup.

Per serving: about
- 225 calories
- 9 g fat
- high source of fiber
- 17 g protein
- 20 g carbohydrate
- excellent source of calcium

Winter Vegetable Soup

2 tsp	vegetable oil	10 mL
2 cups	diced peeled potatoes	500 mL
1/2 cup	each chopped onion, carrot and celery	125 mL
2 cups	vegetable stock	500 mL
1 cup	shredded cabbage	250 mL
1 tsp	dried basil	5 mL
1	bay leaf	1
1	can (19 oz/540 mL) tomatoes, chopped	1
1/2 cup	frozen peas	125 mL
1/4 cup	chopped fresh parsley	50 mL
1/4 tsp	each salt and pepper	1 mL
1/3 cup	freshly grated Parmesan cheese	75 mL

● In heavy saucepan, heat oil over medium heat; cook potatoes, onion, carrot and celery, stirring occasionally, for 5 minutes or until onions are softened.

● Add stock, cabbage, basil and bay leaf; bring to boil. Reduce heat, cover and simmer for 15 to 20 minutes or until vegetables are tender.

● Stir in tomatoes, peas, parsley and their juices, salt and pepper; heat until steaming. Discard bay leaf. Ladle into bowls. Sprinkle with cheese. Makes 4 servings.

Use the vegetables listed as a guide, but add others or make substitutions as you like.

Per serving: about
- 190 calories
- 8 g fat
- high source of fiber
- 8 g protein
- 28 g carbohydrate
- good source of calcium

Broccoli and Potato Chowder

Here's one delicious and easy soup any culinary debutante can cook up.

Per serving: about
- 325 calories
- 19 g fat
- high source of fiber
- 13 g protein
- 27 g carbohydrate
- good source of iron

4 cups	chicken or vegetable stock	1 L
2	carrots, diced	2
1	onion, chopped	1
1	large potato, peeled and diced	1
1	stalk celery, sliced	1
4 cups	chopped broccoli (about 1 bunch)	1 L
3 tbsp	all-purpose flour	50 mL
2 tbsp	butter, softened	25 mL
1/2 cup	(approx) milk	125 mL
1	pkg (125 g) herbed cream cheese, cubed	1
1 tbsp	chopped fresh dill or parsley	15 mL

● In large saucepan, bring stock to boil. Add carrots, onion, potato and celery; return to boil. Reduce heat and simmer for about 10 minutes or until vegetables are tender.

● Add broccoli; return to boil. Reduce heat, cover and simmer for 5 minutes or until tender-crisp. In small bowl and using fork, blend flour with butter until smooth. Return soup to boil, gradually stirring in flour mixture; boil, stirring, for 1 minute.

● Add 1/2 cup (125 mL) milk; bring just to simmer. Stir in cream cheese; simmer, stirring, just until cheese is melted. Add more milk to thin, if desired. Ladle into bowls. Sprinkle with dill. Makes 4 servings.

Corn Chowder

Creamed corn does not contain cream, but it still provides the satisfying richness and substance that's so necessary when soup is supper. You can vary the vegetables, depending on the crop in your crisper.

Per serving: about
- 270 calories
- 5 g fat
- high source of fiber
- 10 g protein
- 53 g carbohydrate

1 tsp	olive oil	5 mL
1	small onion, chopped	1
1	potato, peeled and diced	1
1	stalk celery, chopped	1
1/4 cup	diced sweet red pepper	50 mL
Pinch	hot pepper flakes	Pinch
1 cup	chicken stock	250 mL
1/2 cup	1% milk	125 mL
1	can (10 oz/284 mL) creamed corn	1
1/4 cup	frozen corn kernels	50 mL
1/4 tsp	each salt and pepper	1 mL
1 tbsp	chopped fresh coriander, basil, thyme or parsley	15 mL

● In heavy saucepan, heat oil over medium heat; cover and cook onion, potato, celery, red pepper and hot pepper flakes, stirring often, for 5 minutes.

● Pour in stock and bring to boil; reduce heat and simmer, covered, for 10 minutes or until potato is tender.

● Add milk, creamed corn, frozen corn, salt and pepper; heat gently until steaming. Ladle into bowls. Sprinkle with coriander. Makes 2 servings.

Bean and Pasta Chowder

When it comes to convenience, canned beans and stewed tomatoes are tops.

Per serving: about
- 145 calories
- 1 g fat
- very high source of fiber
- 8 g protein
- 30 g carbohydrate

1	can (8 oz/227 mL) beans in tomato sauce	1
1	can (10 oz/284 mL) stewed tomatoes, coarsely chopped	1
1 cup	chicken or vegetable stock	250 mL
1/4 cup	small pasta shells	50 mL
	Pepper	

● In saucepan, bring beans, tomatoes and their juices and stock to boil, stirring occasionally.

● Add pasta; reduce heat to medium and boil gently, stirring several times, for about 18 minutes or just until pasta is tender but firm. Season with pepper to taste. Makes 3 servings.

Curried Cauliflower and Tofu Soup ▲

8 oz	firm tofu	250 g
1/4 cup	butter	50 mL
1	cauliflower, cut in florets	1
2	onions, chopped	2
2	cloves garlic, minced	2
3	carrots, finely diced	3
2	potatoes, peeled and finely diced	2
2 tsp	each ground cumin, coriander and curry powder	10 mL
5 cups	chicken or vegetable stock	1.25 L
1 tsp	salt	5 mL
1 cup	frozen peas	250 mL
1/4 cup	chopped fresh parsley	50 mL

● Cut tofu into 1/2-inch (1 cm) cubes; set aside.

● In large saucepan, melt butter over medium heat; cook cauliflower, onions, garlic, carrots and potatoes, stirring occasionally, for 5 minutes.

● Stir in cumin, coriander and curry powder; cook, stirring, for 1 minute. Stir in stock and salt; bring to boil. Reduce heat, cover and simmer until vegetables are tender, about 8 minutes.

● Stir in tofu and peas; simmer for 1 to 2 minutes or until heated through. Ladle into bowls. Sprinkle with parsley. Makes 6 servings.

Firm tofu is highly nutritious and a dream to cook with. Here, it slips into a soup, but it can also be cubed and added to a meatless tomato sauce, pasta or other salads or vegetable stews.

Per serving: about
- 270 calories
- 13 g fat
- excellent source of iron
- 15 g protein
- 27 g carbohydrate
- very high source of fiber

Quick-Supper Basics

GREENS

No time to cook a side vegetable? Toss a salad or offer raw carrot, celery, broccoli and rutabaga sticks, instead.

● On your shopping list, plan for a salad per supper. Buy Bibb or Boston lettuce, romaine and leaf lettuce, mushrooms, cucumber, watercress, sprouts and arugula to enjoy soon after shopping.

● For later in the week, buy cabbage, celery, fennel, radishes, carrots, Belgian endive, radicchio, hard avocados and not-quite-red tomatoes.

● Difficult as it is to do, ready your leafy greens when you get home from shopping. Rinse, spin-dry and wrap in clean kitchen towels before enclosing in plastic bags and storing in the crisper.

● Store mushrooms in paper bag in crisper.

● Let tomatoes and avocados ripen at room temperature out of sunlight.

● Investigate some of the ready-to-toss salad mixes available at your local supermarket. Formerly just slaw fixings, these now include tender baby leaves and more exotic greens such as oak leaf lettuce, mitzuna or arugula.

● Whisk up a low-fat dressing that will last a few days.

GRAINS

You don't have to resort to instant rice to include the all-important grain part of your meal.

● Remember, *Canada's Food Guide to Healthy Eating* stresses that grains or grain products such as rice, barley, bulgur, couscous, bread, breakfast cereals and pasta are the most important part of your diet, and we should be having between five and twelve servings each and every day. That sounds like a lot, but it really isn't, given that half a bagel, a slice of bread, a cup (250 mL) of pasta, a half cup (125 mL) of cooked rice or even a modest bowl of rice is considered a "serving."

● Plan on bread or buns to go with supper or stews. Pick them up fresh or freeze your selection when you get home from shopping. Heating in the oven takes just minutes and adds to the appeal.

● When cooking rice, pasta or potatoes one night, make enough for an encore the following evening. The second time around, reheat, freshen up with a toss of herbs, include in a new recipe such as fried rice, baked pasta or dress in a salad.

VEGETABLES

The produce department has quick suppers and busy cooks in mind:

● Stir-fry vegetables come in a mix.

● Salad-bar selections include broccoli and cauliflower florets. They're certainly more expensive than buying your own head or bunches, but there's no waste and they're ready to go in the pot or to use as dippers.

● The mushrooms are sliced.

● Minicarrots are peeled and ready to steam.

● Spinach, the old standby, is increasingly pot-ready, especially crinkly-leaf Savoy variety, and needs just a quick rinse in lukewarm water to release any soil.

● To steam vegetables — a no-fuss way is to prepare a variety all at once — bring about 2 inches (5 cm) of water to boil in a large saucepan. Insert steamer rack (or use colander or metal sieve) and start with hardest vegetables, such as potatoes, carrots, rutabaga, squash, parsnips and onions. Steam until almost tender, about 20 minutes, before adding quicker-cooking vegetables

such as beans, broccoli, cauliflower, broccoflower that take an additional 10 minutes. Or, in the last few minutes, add the truly quick cookers such as spinach, Swiss chard, beet greens, rapini, sugar snap peas, shelled peas or snow peas.

DESSERTS

You don't need to do a lot of baking to end a meal with a sweet yet healthful flourish. If you do bake cookies, choose the drop variety or healthful squares such as date.

● Really good fresh fruit can't be beat as a sweet finale to a meal, and if your crisper and fruit bowl are stocked you're home-free.

● Fruit helps you get your fiber and vitamin quota, and five to ten servings daily are recommended in *Canada's Food Guide to Healthy Eating.*

● Aim for fruit in season — berries in the spring and early summer; peaches, nectarines, apricots and plums in August; grapes, apples and pears in the fall.

● Year-round frozen berries make an excellent sauce for low-fat frozen yogurt, no-fat fruit sorbets and light ice creams. Buzz up some frozen fruit with yogurt for a quick yogurt slush.

● And then there are bananas — pretty nice when ripe, sliced over yogurt and drizzled with maple syrup.

● A dried apricot, date, fig or prune is an amazingly delicious way to satisfy a craving for something sweet.

● Don't overlook fruit canned in its own juices. Pears, peaches, pineapple and fruit salad especially are a real treat.

● Applesauce and stewed rhubarb are old standbys whose appeal has not dated.

● Fruit crisps and crumbles are quick to put together and impress even the most sophisticated palates.

The Contributors

Canadian Living Test Kitchen

In the Canadian Living Test Kitchen. From left: Kate Gammal, Susan Van Hezewijk, Donna Bartolini (Test Kitchen manager), Jennifer MacKenzie, Daphna Rabinovitch (associate food editor) and Elizabeth Baird (food director).

Photography Credits

FRED BIRD: pages 61, 85.

DOUGLAS BRADSHAW:
    pages 7, 21, 54, 57, 65,
    76, 80, 86.

CLIVE CHAMPION:
    front cover.

MICHAEL MAHOVLICH:
    pages 39, 40.

VINCE NOGUCHI: page 10.

CURTIS TRENT: photo of
    Elizabeth Baird and Test
    Kitchen staff.

MICHAEL WARING:
    pages 4, 17, 25, 43, 44,
    49, 69, 73, 74.

ROBERT WIGINGTON:
    pages 12, 18, 23, 29, 35,
    37, 47, 52, 58, 67, 70, 79.

Special thanks to Douglas
Bradshaw for providing the
inspiration for the front-
cover photograph.

Index

Special Thanks

We at *Canadian Living* appreciate the continuing commitment to *Canadian Living's Best* series by Random House of Canada, and particularly the enthusiastic support of president and publisher David Kent and mass marketing sales manager (Ballantine Books) Duncan Shields.

Our magazine and cookbook motto is "Tested Till Perfect" and for that, a vote of thanks to Daphna Rabinovitch, who is also our associate food editor, and to the Test Kitchen staff — Kate Gammal, Heather Howe, Jennifer MacKenzie and Susan Van Hezewijk — under recently appointed manager Donna Bartolini. Thanks also to our food writers, including Margaret Fraser, Carol Ferguson, Anne Lindsay, Jan Main, Dana McCauley, Beth Moffatt, Rose Murray, Iris Raven and Bonnie Stern.

On the editorial side, we are indebted to *Canadian Living*'s senior editors Beverley Renahan, Julia Armstrong and, until recently, Donna Paris, who make sure all recipes are consistent in style and easy to understand — and to Madison Press editors Wanda Nowakowska and Beverley Sotolov for seeing this project through all its editorial stages. Thanks also to Olga Goncalves and Tina Gaudino for their invaluable help behind the scenes.

For the beautiful style and appealing photographs featured in every *Canadian Living's Best* cookbook, our thanks to former creative directors Martha Weaver and Deborah Fadden and to food photographers Fred Bird, Douglas Bradshaw, Clive Champion, Vincent Noguchi, Michael Mahovlich, Michael Waring and Robert Wigington. Food and props stylists also contribute enormously to the appetizing results, and we gratefully acknowledge food stylists Kate Bush, Ruth Gangbar, Jennifer McLagan, Claire Stancer and Olga Truchan, and prop stylists Maggi Jones, Patty LaCroix, Shelly Vlahantones and Janet Walkinshaw. We are also indebted to designer Gord Sibley and his assistant, Dale Vokey, for the wonderful design of the series.

Appreciation is in order for our editor-in-chief, Bonnie Cowan, and our publisher, Caren King, who stand behind the whole food department's vision and passion for great Canadian food.

Elizabeth Baird

Over 100 delicious recipes — in no time at all!

Look to
CANADIAN LIVING
for all of the
best

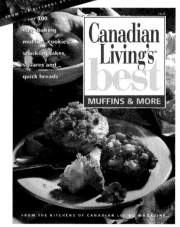

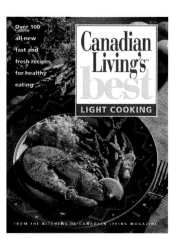

Over 100 all-new fast and fresh recipes for healthy eating

Over 100 great-tasting ways to serve this family favorite

Over 100 satisfying stews, soups, casseroles, stir-fries and more

Over 100 easy-baking muffins, cookies, snacking cakes, squares and quick breads

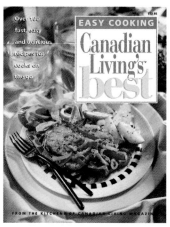

Over 100 all-new recipes for main dishes, salads, sauces and soups

Over 100 all-new recipes for perfect meals around the grill

Over 100 fast, easy and delicious recipes for cooks on the go

Over 100 recipes for garden-fresh entrées, salads, side dishes and soups

Watch for more new books in the months ahead...
from Canadian Living so you know they're —THE BEST!